Praise fo

"Jurgen is one of the world's great young leaders. In his book *PUSH*, Jurgen instructs and inspires us all to believe that God has more planned for us than we could ever imagine and to not give up until we see all that God has in store for us."

BENNY PEREZ, LEAD PASTOR,

WWW.THECHURCHLV.COM

"*PUSH: Pray Until Something Happens* is an important book that encourages us all to embrace the true power of prayer. This is a book that will push YOU to take action and keep praying to become the blessing you were meant to be."

PASTOR TOMMY BARNETT, CO-PASTOR,

PHOENIX FIRST; FOUNDER, L.A. AND

PHOENIX DREAM CENTERS

"One of the greatest challenges of our day is how to present timeless orthodoxy and truths to a somewhat seasonal and transient generation. Jurgen Matthesius has not only taken that challenge but has risen to the occasion! Not everyone can cause the new believer and the Gospel veteran to take a fresh look at prayer in such a way that both are inspired, challenged, and changed. If God is talking to you about prayer, or if you are talking to others about prayer, *PUSH* is your book and this is your time."

MICHAEL S. PITTS, FOUNDER,

CORNERSTONE CHURCH, TOLEDO, OH;

BISHOP, CORNERSTONE GLOBAL NETWORK

"What an appropriate acronym for prayer—*PUSH: Pray Until Something Happens*. This is what prayer is all about. As you read this book, you will be rewarded with a renewed passion to pray more fervently and effectively."

KONG HEE, FOUNDER/SENIOR PASTOR,

CITY HARVEST CHURCH, SINGAPORE

"Through diligent biblical study and reflection, *PUSH* calls into the light many truths about prayer and our roles in it. We are all destined for great things, and if we are to obey God and truly live in His will, it is time we take responsibility for our actions and embrace the power He has given us."

PASTOR MATTHEW BARNETT,
SENIOR PASTOR, ANGELUS TEMPLE;
COFOUNDER, THE DREAM CENTER

"As you read through these pages you will be pushed and challenged to take your prayer life to the next level. Full of practical insights and relatable stories, this book will equip you with the tools needed to pray more effectively as well as stir within you an excitement for prayer."

LISA BEVERE, MESSENGER INTERNATIONAL,
BEST-SELLING AUTHOR/MINISTER, *KISSED
THE GIRLS AND MADE THEM CRY, FIGHT
LIKE A GIRL*, AND *LIONESS ARISING*

"Jurgen is one of the finest communicators I know and his book *PUSH* is a great example of his life and ministry. I would highly recommend this book to anyone who wants to take territory and advance their life and the Kingdom."

PASTOR STEVE KELLY, SENIOR PASTOR,
WAVE CHURCH, VIRGINIA BEACH

"Well it is about time! It's about time an authentic man of God stood up and declared truth into an often bewildered and confused generation of Christians. Too often when it comes to prayer, we can be like the Israelites of old, wandering aimlessly in the desert. But God directs our steps and guides our way to the promised land. Jurgen beautifully highlights this path and points us in a direction that is clear and easy to follow. *PUSH* is creative, practical, and packed full of wisdom. If you really want to take God seriously, then get ready to have all your buttons pushed!"

DR. ROBI SONDEREGGER, OXYGEN
INSTITUTE, SWITZERLAND

PUSH

PRAY UNTIL SOMETHING

HAPPENS

PUSH

PRAY UNTIL SOMETHING HAPPENS

DIVINE PRINCIPLES FOR PRAYING WITH CONFIDENCE,
DISCERNING GOD'S WILL, AND BLESSING OTHERS

JURGEN MATTHESIUS

NELSON
BOOKS

An Imprint of Thomas Nelson

Published in Nashville, Tennessee, by Nelson Books, an imprint of Thomas Nelson. Nelson Books and Thomas Nelson are registered trademarks of HarperCollins Christian Publishing, Inc.

Published in association with the literary agency of The Fedd Agency, Post Office Box 341973, Austin, TX 78734.

Thomas Nelson, Inc., titles may be purchased in bulk for educational, business, fund-raising, or sales promotional use. For information, please e-mail SpecialMarkets@ThomasNelson.com.

The Library of Congress Cataloging-in-Publication Data is on file with the Library of Congress

ISBN-13: 9781400206513

Printed in the United States of America

14 15 16 17 18 RRD 6 5 4 3

To my wife, Leanne, for her amazing wisdom and the way she continually challenges me to become a better man, husband, father, and—above all—follower of Christ!

Also to my mother- and father-in-law, Alan and Valerie Grey. Your love for me the last twenty-three years has meant the world to me. Your wisdom and example have allowed me to reshape my life into something that is so much more Christlike. Thank you.

To my children: Jordan, Ash, Tommy, and Zoe. You grow up so fast, and it has been a delight beyond words to be trusted by the Lord to raise you. I love you with all my heart.

To my pastors, Phil and Christine Pringle, for your amazing love, faith, and support all these years. I owe so much of who I am and what I carry to you!

And finally, to my amazing church, staff, and team here at C3 San Diego! Fighting for the soul of a city with you is a privilege and blessing from heaven.

Contents

Foreword

The book of Jeremiah speaks of men who are valiant for truth on the earth. My friend, Pastor Jurgen Matthesius, is one such man. As you will discover in the following pages, he has a passion for you to understand who God is, how He works, and how you can partner with Him to impact your world of influence.

Many miss the plan of God for their lives because of wrong thinking and wrong believing about His activity in our world. When they are unable to reconcile the idea of a loving, all-powerful God to the evil they see and experience, they reject Him or form false doctrines to explain what they think is His behavior. In either case, they become ineffective servants of God, and more sadly still, they distance themselves from the intimate friendship He desires to have with them. The critical revelation that would keep them from straying—and that will keep you firmly established in Him no matter what you face—is not only that God can bring light into the darkness, but that He has already done so by empowering us with the Spirit and authority of His Son.

Jesus said that knowledge of the truth is what sets us free. As you read *PUSH*, I believe you will find more freedom than ever before to pray with conviction, receive the word of God in resolute faith, and advance the kingdom of God in any circumstance. The understanding of your power and position in Christ that you are about to receive through this message has the potential to change your life forever. The good news in a time of suffering and uncertainty is that God's will can be known, it is good, and it absolutely can come to pass. As you learn to actively participate in the work of God, you will see His glory displayed and the plans of the enemy routed from your life.

I know that many hours of labor and prayer have gone into preparing this word for you, and I believe that the seed about to be sown in your life will bear much fruit. Open your heart to the Holy Spirit and prepare yourself to receive all that God has for you.

John Bevere, author / speaker

Messenger International

Colorado Springs / United Kingdom /

Australia

Introduction

Of all human endeavors, virtually nothing compares to the activity of prayer.

Prayer directly connects that which is mortal and temporary to that which is divine and eternal. There are two distinct aspects of prayer: communion with the Almighty, and the exercise of dominion over the earth.

This book will touch on the former but will prioritize the latter. Not that the former is not important—it is vital—but there are already many books that have been written on prayer from an intimacy and relational aspect; however, very few have been written on its avail of divine power to live victoriously in this life.

I have sought to destroy many of the religious myths handed down to us from previous generations and expose to you what the Bible teaches and instructs on this powerful privilege that we have. I want to enable you to conquer those forces that seek to conquer you.

PUSH is simply an acronym for "Pray Until Something Happens." Much has been lost in the art of "tarrying" in prayer because of our instant-access generation. We find our impatient selves in the McDonald's drive-thru hitting the steering wheel with jeers of "Come on, come on, how long is this going to take?"

when we have been there a full three minutes while the good folks inside cook dinner for our entire family. If I need an answer to a tough question I simply go online and ask "The All-Knowing Mr. Google," who not only gives me more than a hundred answers to select from but also states how instantly he was able to search for, acquire, and send me that information (often in one second or less!).

Yet the Bible does not teach prayer this way. A conflict therefore exists between the "instant generation" and breakthrough in prayer, with the danger looming of a generation losing heart or, worse still, giving up on prayer because it didn't work (immediately)!

What if Elijah had given up on the fifth or sixth time he prayed for the Lord to send rain? What if Jesus prayed only once in the Garden of Gethsemane instead of three times with such intensity that He literally sweated drops of blood? Would He have been able to make the decision to endure all that lay before Him to save mankind? I shudder to think.

No my friend, *PUSH* seeks to put a spotlight on the biblical truths around the power of effective prayer that somehow have been lost in too many circles today and must be rediscovered by the emerging generation. God is faithful. He is just waiting for us to be willing to "Pray Until Something Happens"!

I realize the audacity of what I am choosing to write about. I am not attempting to be belligerent or arrogant, but I also will not neglect to present biblical truths that for some reason do not make it into the doctrinal lineup in our current menu of Sunday liturgy. These are truths I believe have been shown to me by the Holy Spirit through years of walking with the Lord and being in desperate situations where I needed the Bible to work or I was sunk.

I have no doubt that this book is going to bring up as many questions as it seeks to answer. You may even come to the conclusion that I titled this book *PUSH* because I am pushing all your buttons! But my intention is only to challenge your current paradigms when it comes to prayer, faith, sovereignty, and the will of God.

Insanity has been described as doing the same thing over and over while expecting a different result. Without even realizing it, we slip into these ruts where we seem stuck, and helplessness or hopelessness sets in. I honestly believe the words of Jesus when He said, "With God all things are possible" (Matt. 19:26). So instead, please see this book as a pleasant tonic to the symptoms of poor doctrine. Trust me; you will not see God, prayer, and life the same again after reading this book.

The genesis of this book largely came out of a tragedy I experienced a number of years ago early in my pastorate in San Diego. I received an urgent call from a new couple in our church who had friends who attended another church who were facing a tremendous tragedy. I raced to the hospital room where I was greeted with a young child fighting for his life. My friends told me as I entered that the reason they had asked me to come was because this family went to a church where they believed that God no longer does miracles. That all these things passed away in the first century. His parents were overwhelmed with helplessness and hopelessness at the sight of their little boy lying on a bed covered in tubes and surrounded by equipment that beeped and buzzed, generating numbers that meant as much as hieroglyphics to the average person.

I stood and wept as I changed places with them in my mind, seeing my son instead of theirs fighting for his little life. We had seen God perform a wonderful miracle just a few months earlier with a young boy who was almost the identical age in an identical situation. The doctors wanted to pull the plug, saying the child was brain dead and would not live, and yet today this young boy is running, playing, walking, talking, and very much alive. As I began to pray, the father of the child interrupted me, chiding me for my "supposed" arrogance for believing in a miracle, and then declared that "this was God's will because they had already prayed three times and nothing happened, therefore this must be God's will and they just needed to accept it." I immediately recognized why their church seldom sees miracles and healings. It is because of an epidemic of what is known as "the New Calvinism" that has become the dominant disposition of a Christianity fraught with pain and disappointment.

On May 12, 2009, *TIME* magazine featured an article on "the New Calvinism" in the section "10 Ideas Changing the World Right Now!" As I read that article, I recognized a teaching that was crippling the church in the United States and around the world, because its core belief inadvertently renders prayer void and useless. Five-point Calvinism believes that due to the "total depravity of man" (the first point), man has no effect on God or His will and certainly plays no part in influencing the Almighty in any way. Therefore everything that happens is God's will.[1]

This doctrine believes that nothing happens outside of His will, so there's no point getting worked up. If God wants something to change, then it will; and if not, just relax—it's all for His glory.

Even though this debate has raged between Calvinists and

Armenians for a few centuries now, *PUSH* is not joining the fray of arguing one side over the other but rather *PUSH* will present biblical truths that have been highlighted to me in my walk with the Lord that circumnavigate these two viewpoints and present a functioning biblical reality.

Upon finishing the article, I realized that this book, *PUSH,* was given to me as an assignment from the Lord. It was to rescue a generation who, through very destructive theology, were being lulled into apathy and inactivity and seeking to rationalize evil while abdicating any responsibility to pray to make a difference. After all, if *everything* has already been decided why even bother praying? Why such a stinging rebuke, Jesus, to very tired disciples in Gethsemene to tarry with You at least an hour in prayer when *"Que sera, sera – whatever will be, will be!"*

The theologies of men must *always* bow to the entire counsel of the Word of God. If our doctrine or theology conflicts with a scripture in the Bible, then we should throw out our theology and start again. Sadly, too many try to change or overlook the Word of God in order to keep their tradition and theology! "These people draw near to Me with their mouth, and honor Me with their lips, but their heart is far from Me. And in vain they worship Me, teaching as doctrines the commandments of men" (Matt. 15:8–9).

Because I am the son of an East German atheist, a former soldier on the wall separating the Communist East from the capitalist West, prayer was *not* something I was brought up with. I had to learn prayer through trial and error. This book is pretty much me sharing with you things that I've tried and proven in my own life, that are 100 percent consistent with Scripture, and that you can depend upon and build your life upon. Everything I have achieved and received from God in this life has come through the medium of prayer. This book will read more like a mini Bible college on prayer than a motivational pump you up book on prayer. I want you to have a clear and strong foundation for effective, powerful prayer.

There are many definitions of prayer, some of which we will look at shortly, but understand this is not about simply trying to get you to spend more time being spiritual as much as it is about empowering you to become more effective and strategic in prayer and actually begin to see dramatic results! Some people may find this thought offensive, but don't give up reading just yet. I believe you are reading this because you are meant to see more of God's will coming to pass in your life. Some may retort, "You shouldn't put God to the test; we should just pray and believe that something good has taken place even if we don't see any visible signs supporting that." While I absolutely concur we need to pray by faith and not by sight, I also believe the Bible makes it clear that "the effective, fervent prayer of a righteous man avails much" (James 5:16). This means visible as well as measurable!

For God's great purposes to be fulfilled in our lives and His will to be established on earth, I need to show you a powerful formula revealed in the Bible that was the inspiration behind the title of this book. Some of the keys we will cover are:

- What the will of God is (and isn't)
- The power and position of God's Word
- How the will of God comes to pass
- What role prayer plays in the process

- What the resistance or opposition is
- Evil forces engaged
- Power tools that are available

God always looks for a person to partner with Him to bring forth His will on earth. There is no such thing as an authority vacuum. We simply replace one authority with another. Our call as Christians is to replace the evil, despot authority of the devil with the gracious, benevolent authority of God through prayer. It doesn't just happen naturally; it must be established manually.

Once I had the catalyst from the Lord for writing a book on prayer and discovering God's will, I found that I lacked a title. What would I call it? Better still, what did God want to call it?

I was heading to the bank thinking about the title, and pulling into the parking lot when I noticed an older lady fussing at the door; she was shaking the handle and groaning like a WWF wrestler who had just been hit in the head by a chair. I immediately thought the bank must be closed.

I looked at my watch. It was a quarter after ten in the morning, so surely the bank wasn't closed. I got out of my car and, as I approached the doors, I could see the lights on and the bank staff going about their business. *Strange*, I thought. Just then, the sweet old lady grabbed the door one more time and strenuously yanked it toward her, groaning like those weight lifters doing squats at the gym. *Could they have forgotten to unlock the door?* I wondered. But upon looking at the door a little more closely, I read the word *Push*. And with that I gave it a gentle push, and the door opened. The little old lady gave me a surprised Forrest Gump look as if to say,

"Lieutenant Dan, you've got a magic door!" Nope, nothing magic about it. The bank was open, but she was pulling when the sign said Push!

Just then I thought I felt the Lord speak to me and say, *So many people are frustratingly pulling and yanking and heaving and sighing at things when they just need to push.* Just like that, I had the title for this book!

It's time to stop being frustrated and worn out by futile activities that yield few kingdom results. It's time to learn how to *push* into God's perfect will and see heaven come to earth in and through your life. Revelation 4:1 says, "After these things I looked, and behold, a *door standing open in heaven.* And the first voice which I heard was like a trumpet speaking with me, saying, 'Come up here, and I will show you things which must take place after this'" (emphasis added). Heaven has a door open to you, but you may need to push to get into what God has for you!

What do Martin Luther King Jr., Winston Churchill, Nelson Mandela, Mother Teresa, Rosa Parks, and William Wilberforce all have in common? They were all people who realized that something does not happen just because it is *right*—it must be accessed by PUSH. The law of entropy tells us that things don't stay as they are; they get progressively worse. A garden develops weeds, energy dissipates, coffee gets cold, rooms get messier, cars rust, love depletes, and passion subsides. All of these things require action to improve them. We live in a world where good and right are not automatic, and God's will on earth must be fought for and pushed into. Get ready to get your push on!

ONE

Zero Gravity

Intercession is truly universal work for the Christian. No place is closed to intercessory prayer. No continent, no nation, no organization, no city, no office. There is no power on earth that can keep intercession out.
—RICHARD HALVERSON

Recently I received a flyer about a new place in town that offered a Zero Gravity experience. The advertisement read "Experience weightlessness, float like an astronaut, fly like a superhero . . ." *Wow*, I thought, *who doesn't want to float like an astronaut; who doesn't want to fly like a superhero? Who doesn't want to experience the euphoria of weightlessness?* It was a ZERO-G experience similar to the ones used to prepare our astronauts for flying into outer space.

As I thought about how much fun it would be, I felt God impress upon me that this is specifically what prayer is *meant* to achieve, experiencing the weightlessness that is accessed through the power of prayer alone.

We are called to cast all of our cares upon Him (Christ) for

He cares for us (1 Peter 5:7). In other words, we will have cares but God says, *I don't want you to be weighed down by those things; instead, I want you to experience weightlessness on a regular basis. I've got this!* We are to feel the Spirit's power lift us up so we float like an astronaut and fly like a superhero through all of life's ups and downs. Weightlessness in the midst of our challenges is the end result of prayer.

> The LORD will extend your mighty scepter from Zion, saying,
> "Rule in the midst of your enemies!" (Ps. 110:2 NIV)

I awoke with a jolt, like when you have one of those freaky dreams that you're falling. My foot had slipped out from underneath the covers, waking me to the reality that I was in the southern regions of New Zealand on a very crisp, cold winter morn. I had just finished ministering at a phenomenal youth camp for one of New Zealand's premier churches, and to say I was completely spent would be an understatement. I was exhausted but satisfied from seeing so many young people respond to the gospel of Christ! It's the only way I know how to minister. I like to give everything I have and leave nothing on the table. Indebted to a Savior who gave His all for me, the least I can do is give the young people entrusted to me by my Savior a "boots and all" gospel presentation.

Youth camps are notorious for many things, sleep deprivation being one of them. After debriefing with the youth pastor and chatting well into the early hours of the morning, I was zonked and ready for bed. So it was no surprise after waking up with a freezing foot that I was keen to bring my limb back under the covers where it was nice and warm. I desperately longed to get back to sleep since I had to be up by seven in order to make the flight home to my wife and children. But I was woken again not even an hour later, not by an exposed limb, but rather by the Holy Spirit prompting me, *Get up and pray!*

You have got to be kidding! was my response. *Surely you have someone else who can get up and pray? I mean, there are more than six billion people on our planet, and while I am flattered that You have come to depend on me to be Your intercessor, surely there is at least one other person You can find who will get up and pray at this hour!* My reasoning was that I had poured out and given my all, from early in the morning until late at night, for the entire weekend. I just wanted to sleep—no, scratch that—I *needed* to sleep. I was heading home and wanted to give my family more than an empty tank, more than a husband and a father who was spent and had nothing left for them.

But the Holy Spirit was persistent: *Get up and pray. Get up and pray.* I thought, *I'm never going to win an argument with God—the Bible says He neither sleeps nor slumbers, so if it comes to a battle of endurance, He has an unfair advantage right there. Okay, I'll get up for fifteen minutes, pray, get it over and done with, make Him happy, then get back into bed. This little "obedience test" of His will get me another pass and keep me in His good books.*

It felt like I was stepping outside into the cold as I slipped out from under the duvet and began to pray. I was so tired, and after about ten minutes of prayer, I knew there was something burning on God's heart, and I knew it would take more than five minutes to get this one across the line. But I ignored the burden I could feel in my spirit, did my fifteen minutes, then climbed back into bed. Ah, the euphoria of getting back into the warm bed, under the duvet and out of the cold—it was like falling face-first into a giant cup of happiness.

But before I could go to sleep, the Holy Spirit came again and said, *Get up and pray!* Now I was annoyed.

You've got to be kidding! Come on! Surely you can get someone else? Please, I just want to sleep!

He just repeated Himself. *Get up and pray!* I could sense there was an urgency in His request, but I was done—starving kids in Africa, war in the Middle East, a lost puppy, I don't care—*someone else can pray!* So I petitioned God, *What is sooooo important that I have to get up and pray right here, right now? You are God—why can't You find someone else to pray for this burden? What is it that's sooooo flipping urgent?* I was beyond pleasantries and for the life of me couldn't figure out why I needed to get up.

Then it hit me like a punch in the face from Mike Tyson: *Get up and pray. Something's wrong with your plane!* Now you've got my attention. *My plane?* I'm not afraid of flying; it doesn't scare me one bit. Crashing is what freaks me out.

I was up and praying with more gusto and fervency than a finalist on *The Biggest Loser*. For the next seventy-five minutes a knot in my stomach prevented me from slipping back into bed or yielding to fatigue when my vocabulary began to run out. I knew I needed to pray, and when all my English and memory verses ran dry, I yielded to allowing the Holy Spirit to pray through me in my heavenly prayer language.

By the time the knot in my stomach dissolved, it was ten

minutes before seven. No time for bed; it was time to shower, have breakfast, and make my way to the airport.

After we arrived at the airport and checked in, the youth pastor suggested we grab coffee. We sat at a large picture window overlooking the runway and had a full view of the planes, specifically my plane. I remember sitting there sipping my cappuccino and thinking to myself, *There's nothing wrong with that plane; it looks completely intact like all the other planes!* Then, *Am I going nuts? Did I just waste a perfectly good night's rest because of fear or anxiety? Was it just mental exhaustion?* The thoughts raced through my mind like bananas in a blender.

I looked at my watch; it was 9:15. The boarding call would come momentarily. But it didn't. Nine thirty came. Then 9:45, and then our flight time of 9:50 came and went. Something was not right.

I saw two engineers dressed in navy blue overalls walk under the plane and go inside the fuselage. After about fifteen minutes they emerged, walked back toward the gate, and disappeared out of sight. Then a voice came over the intercom: "Ladies and gentlemen, unfortunately there is a mechanical problem with this flight, and the plane is not fit for service. We apologize for the delay, but we are going to have to fly another plane up from Wellington to get you to Auckland." The announcement was met with groans of disappointment and frustration, the passengers obviously upset that they would now be late for their appointments, their meetings, or their loved ones waiting for them.

The airline decided to move the plane from the gate. But just as the engines were fired up, *BOOM!* One of the engines on the wing completely erupted into flames! Fire trucks arrived to put out the blaze. Little children excitedly pushed their way to the windows with "oohs" and "aahs." The elderly folk, not to be outdone, also crammed their way toward the glass to observe and provide their own commentary on the unfolding activity.

A shudder went through my body like an electric current. *What if I hadn't prayed? What if I had stayed in bed where it was warm and ignored the voice of God?* Could God have gotten someone else up to pray? Yes, quite possibly, but they would have had to be *very* faithful to His leading and promptings, as this wasn't their flight; it was mine. I realized then that everything that happens to bring about the perfect will of God on the earth does so on the backs and labor of the faithful. If that engine had exploded and caught fire midway through our flight, what would have been the likelihood of the pilots landing the plane somewhere safely? It seemed more likely that crashing and fatalities would have been the outcome, as I'm not sure how much a pilot can do with one engine completely gone and a wing on fire. I knew my decision to get up and pray—and pray fervently, until the knot in my stomach relaxed—was probably the best decision I had made in a very long time.

Two hours later we were in the air on a brand-new plane, and I couldn't help but laugh to myself as I heard the other passengers around me complaining about how late they were going to be and what an inconvenience it all was. All I could think was, *Well, people, if someone hadn't prayed this morning, maybe we wouldn't have the ability to complain; being inconvenienced is always better than being dead!* I immediately saw just how important obedience is in accomplishing God's will. It was an incredible lesson, one that lingers with me to this day. God is able to perform powerful miracles when He is able to find someone willing to put his or her comfort second to His call. Remember, the only ability God looks for in man is "avail-ability"!

Prayer is the conveyor system that transports things from one dimension into another. God's will in heaven travels into the terrestrial realm here on earth through the medium of prayer. A baby is not born into the world without some push taking place. Likewise, for us to go from a small, confined place into a larger, brighter one, we need to learn how to push in prayer.

Prayer shifts things from one dimension to another, but it also does something even more magnificent: it leverages the power of God in our lives. Prayer is direct access to the most powerful being in the universe. No one is like Him. None compares to Him, and there is none beside Him. PUSH prayer is the invitation of God to access His strength in our lives for whatever we face. Much like a young child asks his father to help lift a weighty object too heavy for his small frame, we are invited to come to our heavenly Father and access His unlimited strength!

Your Time Is Up, Mr. Suharto!

Let me take you back to the year 1998. The location was Jakarta, Indonesia. President Suharto enjoyed uninterrupted power as the nation's president. However, his regime had slain more than a million people who voiced opposition to his leadership at some time or another. The country of Indonesia was in financial ruins largely due to the gross corruption and misappropriation of federal funds that Suharto made his personal treasury. Add to that government corruption, unabated consumption, and mounting foreign debt, and inflation soared to the point that most of Indonesia's citizens couldn't afford even the most basic staples. Suharto then squandered much of a $43 billion bailout given by the IMF to help the struggling nation, using the money to line his and his family's pockets. Meanwhile the nation continued to suffer, but with the national military placed firmly in his back pocket, resistance seemed futile and change did not look forthcoming.

As gas and oil prices continued to rise, the pressure of staples being well beyond the reach of the working-class citizens created a murmur among the young, especially the students. But who were they against a tyrant with the full military might at his beck and call? In power since 1966, Suharto's New Order party seemed certain to remain in that position, and most foreign journalists and political commentators believed that Suharto would certainly die in office. However, in May 1998, hundreds of thousands of students protested, occupying the parliament building and other capital city centers throughout the country, calling for the resignation of Suharto.

Suharto had formed a strong, centralized, military-dominated government, with soldiers stationed in every city instilling a deep fear of authority throughout the 3,000 square miles that make up Indonesia. Even though orders were given to the army to disperse the protestors, the young students chanted for change, demanding an end to the corruption and dictatorship. On May 21, 1998, seeing no other recourse and realizing his complete loss of power over his nation, Suharto succumbed to the demands and resigned. Cheers and celebrations filled the streets, and awe filled the news media around the world.

For good to triumph and corruption to end, the students of Indonesia had to unite and push. In fact, every revolution in history has this element associated with it. Nothing shifts unless push is present.

I have written this book out of a personal conviction that the perfect will of God requires us to push against opposing forces, because it does not automatically happen in our lives. I believe that God is not willing that *any* should perish (2 Peter 3:9), and yet this is not sufficient to see everyone turning to God in repentance. I believe that God's perfect will requires acceptance, engagement, and specific activity on our part. I believe our will *must* be engaged first before we can see God's perfect will come to pass.

I also believe that there is a great battle and resistance for "God's will in heaven" to be done here on earth! You are in this battle whether you like it or not. There are no bystanders in this game, and these forces around us are playing for keeps.

I believe that the earth infrequently sees glimpses of God's perfect will coming to pass. These are the moments that fill us with wonder and cause us to be overcome with amazement, thankfulness, and praise. We often call these moments *miracles*. But are these the result of divine intervention alone, or are they the result of intercession and prayer? Does God do what He likes without regard or communication? Sure, He doesn't need to ask anyone for permission, but He did give man dominion over the earth; so does

He involve man in His plans or operate independently? This book will answer that.

I once heard someone say, "I don't believe in miracles, I depend upon them!" I have come to adopt this as my own personal mantra for how I do ministry and life. I believe that as you read this book, it will bring you into a place where the miraculous becomes much more commonplace in your life. God's power is not only available but also reliable. Jesus said, "Most assuredly, I say to you, he who believes in Me, the works that I do he will do also; and greater works than these he will do, because I go to My Father" (John 14:12). In twenty-eight years of following Him, I cannot catalog in one book all the miracles I have seen and experienced. God is good. Always.

Jesus, a Perfect Picture of God

When we look at the life of Jesus Christ—God incarnate—we see God's perfect will in operation. Jesus, unlike other religious figures in history, did not merely speak about the will of God; He actually performed it to the minutest detail. His life, leadership, and example are unmatched in history, stamping His identity as the Son of God beyond the impotent claims of skeptics.

Not only was the life and death of Christ a perfect fulfillment of the will of God but it also delivers great hope, boldly declaring that no matter what we are facing, no matter how dire our circumstances, if we can succeed in engaging God we can see amazing things take place in our lives. We find ourselves no longer just believing in miracles but depending upon them!

Jesus Is Our Example

Jesus constantly had the people of His time marveling and praising God. They saw the dead raised to life. At a wedding they experienced ordinary water turned into the most extraordinary wine. Large crowds witnessed five loaves and two fish turned into a super-sized feast for some five thousand men plus women and children. Blind eyes were opened, storms were calmed, the sea was walked upon, and miracles took place everywhere He went.

These are the things we mere mortals marvel at, and yet Jesus said, "For I have come down from heaven, not to do My own will, but the will of Him who sent Me" (John 6:38). In other words, "*Everything* you see me doing is God's perfect will." That's why we marvel. Heaven is a place of perpetual and spectacular marveling. We will live in an everlasting uninterrupted state of being, continuously in awe of the manifestation of God's perfect will again and again for all eternity. However, here on earth in this life we are engaged in a battle for His will to come to pass. Jesus had to cast out demons because they would not leave voluntarily. Jesus had to lay hands on people and command healing to take place because they would not have recovered themselves. Jesus had to rebuke an insidious, invisible evil force that had momentarily occupied the rhetoric of one of his closest friends, Simon Peter. Jesus showed us by kneeling and sweating drops of blood in the Garden of Gethsemane that He had to continuously PUSH. Yet, Jesus was Himself the answer, deliverer, and the personification of God's will through answered prayer. He embodies the formula for how God's will triumphs in the earth. It may sound irreverent that I have used the word *formula* to describe the working of God's power in the earth, but it is there in the Scripture for us to observe, receive instruction from, and apply to our lives.

Are you ready?

Paul said, "But one thing I do, forgetting those things which are behind and reaching forward to those things which are ahead, I *press toward* the goal for the prize of the upward call of God in Christ Jesus" (Phil. 3:13–14, emphasis added). Are you fed up with being pushed around by the enemy and are now ready to push back? Get ready to go to a whole new level in your walk with God and your experience of all He has for you. It's time to PUSH!

TWO

Inception

*In the beginning was the Word, and the Word
was with God, and the Word was God.*
—JOHN 1:1

Whenever God changes the state of a thing, He uses a wonderfully detectable formula. He does it with His Word. In the beginning God created light by the proclamation of His Word. God speaks to create. When darkness permeated everything we know of in the universe, God simply spoke and His Word brought forth light. God then separated the darkness from the light. The two have co-existed ever since. Jesus is the light of the world because He is the Word of God. The Word of God is light (Ps. 119:105). When we speak the Word of God we invade the darkness of this world creating God's will for light to come to pass.

Jesus came as the Word of God to overcome the darkness (evil), bringing forth salvation for mankind. This is how prayer works. This is God's inception into the Scriptures and into the world in which we live. This is the formula for effective prayer.

In the Hollywood movie *Inception*, from which I derived the title for this chapter, Leonardo DiCaprio plays the role of Dom Cobb, a highly skilled mind thief who breaks into the minds of his victims while they are asleep. Cobb extracts highly confidential information like passwords, PIN numbers, and account information when they are at their most vulnerable, in what the movie describes as the dream state.

In the movie, however, he is asked to do the reverse and instead of extracting information, he is asked to place information in there to cause them to believe something and thereby act upon it. It shows the power of a thought, word, or belief. It shows that all of our beliefs and thoughts must come from an original source. The Bible teaches us to build our thoughts and beliefs on the Word of God. For then we will make our way prosperous, and then we will have good success (Josh. 1:8–9).

When God saw a world that had gone awry, He planted the word deep into it. Jesus is that Word that God sent into the world. Like a seed (Luke 8:11) He was planted in the earth, and adhering to the botanical processes of all the earth, He died, but rose again (or sprouted) on the third day and brought forth a harvest of sons and daughters.

Effective prayer follows a very simple formula. It *must* be Word based, Word led, and Word sustained. Jesus said in Luke 4:4 that "man shall not live by bread alone, but by every word of God." The Bible teaches that God heals and delivers with His Word (Ps. 107:20). It also says that it was the Word that created everything in existence and it's the same word that sustains everything, holding it all together (2 Peter 3:5, 7).

Jesus is not just the centerpiece of history but the centerpiece of all existence; In fact the centerpiece of life itself! We are called to pray in His name. It alone has power over all of creation. Jesus is the Word and when we build our prayers on the Word of God, we are literally unleashing the victorious, conquering, risen Son of God upon our circumstances.

Many years ago, I was approached by a couple at a youth camp in New Zealand who had had several miscarriages and undergone many medical examinations only to constantly receive the negative report that natural childbearing was not possible for them. As I prayed for them I felt compassion, but that alone is not sufficient to make a change. Compassion without power becomes no more than sympathy. As I prayed, I waited for a word from God. Then it came and I spoke it to them. Immediately the atmosphere around this couple shifted. Something was transferred. Something changed.

A year later I was ministering again in New Zealand but in a different part of the country when a young woman approached me and said, "Hey, remember me?" I tried to pretend I knew who she was, but she could see through my bluff. She said, "Last year you prayed for us and told us next year we would be holding a little baby girl." "I said *whaaat*???" I was thinking, *Uh-oh, here comes a lawsuit*, but just then her husband walked over holding a beautiful little girl in his arms and said that they were that couple I prayed for.

PUSH is about learning how to pray using the Word of God as your prophetic tool to bring about God's will on the earth. How do I know I am praying according to God's will? How do I know I am not using the Word of God to manipulate things to bring about my own will? Well, keep reading because this book will address some of the many misnomers surrounding God's will, God's Word, and even prayer itself. Some believe it doesn't matter how we pray; heck, it doesn't even matter *who* we pray to, as long as we pray. Really?

Effective Prayer

The effective, fervent prayer of a righteous man avails much.
(James 5:16)

If effective prayer exists, then there must by necessity be such a thing as ineffective prayer. Jesus taught as much when He spoke the parable of the Pharisee and the tax collector in Luke 18:9–14. One of them prayed in such a way as moving the heart of God toward him and the other prayed in such a way as to block a flow of grace coming toward him. If James 5:16 says that the "fervent prayer of a righteous man avails much," then there must also be prayer that "avails little," to use the New King James vernacular. In fact, taking James 5:16 and applying antonyms would tell us that "the lethargic, passive, disinterested prayers of a sinful or compromising man are of little effect"! A statement like this would seem inflammatory to some, because we do not like the idea that somehow we are responsible for not just who we pray to, but how we pray, and our "credit rating" with the One to whom we are praying.

Yet let me make it very clear: this is exactly the case for effective prayer. If you are praying to the wrong god, your prayers will be worthless because there is only one true God who is all-powerful and full of mercy and compassion. God rebuked the children of Israel through the prophet Jeremiah, telling them that they would be scattered because of their idolatry and would have exactly what they have lusted for: "And there you will serve gods, the work of men's hands, wood and stone, which neither see nor hear nor eat nor smell" (Deut. 4:28).

So it is important to pray to the one true God if we want our prayers to be effective, powerful, and answered. But make no mistake, if we pray prayers that are half-hearted—the empty, passive mumblings of a heart disinterested in the One to whom we are praying—our prayers will be greatly limited.

Lastly, if our prayers come from a place of unworthiness, faithlessness, wickedness, depravity, or sinfulness, we are told that God does not hear us either. Now depending upon your theological background, you may well be saying, "That is pretty much all of us! We are all unworthy, sinful creatures and should not expect a just and holy God to be in any way moved to answer our prayers." A very true statement *if* we are completely ignorant of what Christ accomplished on the cross: "For He made Him who knew no sin to be sin for us, that we might become the righteousness of God in Him" (2 Cor. 5:21).

We can pray from a position that *we* have disqualified ourselves by our sins, our mistakes, and our rebellion, or we can pray from the place that *Christ* has earned (qualified) for us in the completed work of the cross. One sets us up in a position of power when we pray, whereas the other has us defeated before we even utter our first words!

This is the difference between *feelings* and *faith*; it is not a matter of Bible interpretation or doctrinal leanings. The Scriptures are black and white in this area; there is no wiggle room here. That's why the writer of Hebrews goes on to say, "But without faith it is impossible to please Him, for he who comes to God must believe that He is, and that He is a rewarder of those who diligently seek Him" (11:6).

Our feelings may well be the overriding voice in our heads and hearts reminding us of our utter sinfulness and our inability to be what we ought to be before a just and holy God. We may even be persuaded to believe there's really no point; why would God answer my prayers? Or we can understand that we have been given abundant grace and have been seated in Christ in the heavenly places at the right hand of the Father. We can choose to believe that God took our sinfulness and all its punishments and placed them upon His only Son, so that we who once were children of wrath are now beloved sons and daughters, His delight and joy!

We must make sure we do not pray from a place of ignorance but rather from revelation. God knows what He has done for us and God "takes no delight in fools" (Eccl. 5:4 NASB). Some believe that we impress God, earning points with Him when we remind Him of our sins, shortcomings, and utter unworthiness. But remember, God knows exactly what He has accomplished through the blood of His only begotten Son on Calvary; He is completely aware of the priceless sacrifice He has made for our redemption. It would be like my wife coming to me describing the ring on her finger by exaggerating how pathetically small the diamond is, how gold is the most pitiful of all minerals, and how dreadful the craftsmanship of the bridge and crown holding the diamond is. Can you imagine if she did this every time we spoke how dreadful I would feel. Yet God paid a much higher price for my life than I did for a ring upon my wife's finger.

If we pray like this, we are basically saying to Him, "What you did on the cross was insufficient and impotent, unable to change my sinful state before you."

Insulting His sacrifice and work is *not* the place where you want to begin your prayers. Instead, we ought to *thank Him* for what He has done through Jesus Christ upon the cross. "Enter His gates with thanksgiving and His courts with praise" is the biblical prescription given to us to approach His throne (Ps. 100:4 NASB). You get a lot more bees with honey than you do with vinegar!

Jesus' death upon the cross has bestowed upon us His perfect righteousness (right standing) with God. Yes, we were totally unworthy, and yet His love overshadowed our unworthiness. He took our utter sinfulness upon Himself and made the exchange. That is what the cross is, a place of exchange. This is called grace! He died the death we deserved so we can live and experience the life He deserved. It is then from this highly elevated position that we begin to let our petitions be made known to our heavenly Father and see our prayers become effective. Amen!

What Prayer Is Not

So we know that some prayers are ineffective. There are three key influencers for this:

1. The pray-er's belief about *who* God is
2. The pray-er's belief about *who* they are
3. The pray-er's belief of *what* they have been given (spiritual authority)

Christianity is the *only* belief system that answers these three questions conclusively. God Himself is truth. Therefore whatever He speaks is truth. God cannot lie because He doesn't simply *have* truth, but rather He *is* truth (Deut. 32:4). Jesus is truth (John 14:6). The Holy Spirit is the Spirit of truth (John 16:13). Because God's Word is truth, we would be wise to make it the final authority on answering life's most important questions. Three of these questions are: who is God, who are we, and what authority have we been given on the earth?

Jesus said, "Wisdom is justified by all her children" (Luke 7:35). The proof is always in the proverbial pudding, and a quick study of history shows that the greatest nations—those that have afforded prosperity and equity to their people, who have made massive strides in medical advancement, educated the masses, and eradicated poverty—are traditionally known as Christian nations. Like the psalmist said, "Blessed is the nation whose God is the LORD" (33:12).

Other religions like Islam declare Allah to be a god who is lone and has no son or other. He is never portrayed as a father, and love is never associated with him. Of the seventy-something references to Allah in the Qur'an none of them refer to him as either love or father. Rather he is portrayed as a harsh, demanding potentate (Qur'an: S. 112:1–4).

Buddhism declares that there is no personal god, for we all have a god consciousness. We are therefore gods ourselves because we are a part of the universe, which is god in essence (Vairacchedika, 14).

Other religions teach polytheism—that there are many gods, and these are capricious, quarreling, and egocentric beings who demand worship like infantile brats constantly in need of appeasement, who must be convinced or bribed to bestow any benevolence upon their devotees.

Your prayer position is greatly weakened by an incorrect perception of the nature and person of God. If you believe that God is indifferent, impersonal, angry, and uncaring, you are greatly demotivated from pressing in for a breakthrough or even believing in help in times of trouble. You more than likely believe that God has purposed this suffering to punish you for past sins committed in a previous life, and any relief in this present suffering would not "buy" you a better rebirth into the next life (this view is similar to Hinduism).

The truth about God—shown to us in Scripture and further confirmed by the revelation of Jesus Christ—is that God is the Creator of the universe and therefore the sovereign ruler over all. It further reveals Him as our heavenly Father, one who loves us, cares for us, and is ultimately responsible for us. He died upon the cross for our sins, not His. He is our Redeemer, one who so loves mankind that He bought us with His own blood and His own life! These are very important and essential facts to give us a strong foundation for prayer. To PUSH, we must believe that God is not only all-powerful but also that He is a God of justice, righteousness, and loving-kindness. We must believe that He is abundant in grace and mercy, He cares, and He "is our refuge and strength, a very present help in trouble" (Ps. 46:1). Like the writer of Hebrews declares, faith limited only to God existing is insufficient to please God. We must also believe that "He is a rewarder of those who diligently seek Him" (Heb. 11:6).

Anything less and you are not in the right position to push your way into a miracle.

The second important issue that must be addressed is *who we are.* Our understanding of who we are determines our approach to God. In the original motion picture of *The Wizard of Oz*, Dorothy and her subjects come near to Oz but are promptly reminded, "Who dares approach the great and powerful Oz?" Islam teaches that it is man's responsibility to pray (five times a day) but that it is arrogant to expect Allah to hear and answer their prayers, for he is god and they are mere men. Most false religions teach the idea that man is unworthy both to approach God and to be heard by Him and must do something to be accepted.

Some religions teach that we are god, which means we have to save ourselves from our calamity—not great if you find yourself in a plane having lost both its engines, spiraling toward the ground at a thousand miles per hour. "It's OK people, I got this . . . I'm a god," is something you won't be hearing anyone say. But once again the Bible declares: "Let us therefore come boldly to the throne of grace, that we may obtain mercy and find grace to help in time of need" (Heb. 4:16). The Bible clearly states that through Christ you and I have been made "joint heirs" with Christ (Rom. 8:17). Who are we? In Christ we are complete in Him (Col. 2:10)! Complete means lacking nothing, having no imperfection. In Christ God sees us as perfect even though we are not. That's why we must pray in His name and approach in His righteousness, not our own. He has made us complete, perfect, and joint heirs. Let this guide how you ask your heavenly Father for things.

The third issue we must address in order to achieve effective prayer is what we have been given! This is commonly referred to today as spiritual authority. For time's sake I am not going to go into the various teachings and misunderstandings of other religions, but I will point out again the biblical truths and their contrast.

The Bible teaches that God is a God of order, structure, authority, and power. It teaches that God gave man authority and power over the work of His hands (Gen. 1:26–28) and that this authority was lost to Satan, who possessed it until Christ (the second Adam) redeemed it: "Then the devil, taking Him up on a high mountain, showed Him all the kingdoms of the world in a moment of time. And the devil said to Him, *'All this authority I will give You, and their glory; for this has been delivered to me,* and I give it to whomever I wish'" (Luke 4:5–6, emphasis added).

When Jesus defeated Satan by rising from the dead on the third day, the Bible teaches that He conquered death and hell and now possesses the keys to them. The risen Christ declared, "All authority has been given to Me in heaven and on earth. Go therefore and make disciples" (Matt. 28:18–19). Jesus redeemed Adam's lost authority, and it is safe now from the devil's temptations and strategies. What the first Adam failed to hold and be guardian of, the second Adam redeems and holds securely until the end of the age.

The Bible teaches that there is a spiritual hierarchy, which I will go into in much greater depth in the following chapters. But suffice it to say, we have been positioned to sit "above" all other powers because we are seated in Christ: "Even when we were dead in trespasses, made us alive together with Christ (by grace you have been saved), and *raised us up together, and made us sit together in the heavenly places in Christ Jesus*" (Eph. 2:5–6, emphasis added).

Only Christianity establishes the truth about the very real spiritual hierarchy that exists in the heavenly (or spiritual) realm, and only Christianity teaches us that we pray from an exalted, elevated position provided *not* by our own good works, suffering, or disciplines, but rather from the grace extended toward us by God who redeemed us in Christ Jesus. We pray from a seated place in Christ, far above every demonic principality or power! No begging, groveling, or penance required, just faith in all that Christ has accomplished upon the cross to reestablish us into right standing with our loving heavenly Father.

It is more than just praying from an elevated position. In ancient warfare kings and commanders would often locate an elevated vantage point to survey the battle on the field or plain below and have the advantage of vision. From there strategic commands could be passed down to the generals on the battlefield. We not only pray from a place of vision, but even greater than that, we pray from a place of utmost power and authority.

The apostle Paul details in Ephesians where Christ is seated (at the right hand of the Father) and then proceeds to educate us on the fact that we are seated in Christ, in the highest seat of authority in the universe, at the right hand of God. No begging to be done here. The devil does not have more authority than you. Many believers, scholars, and Bible teachers will tell you correctly that the devil is more powerful than you. He is a supernatural being, an angel of the highest order, and he possesses great power. However, power is different from authority. You have been placed in a seat of authority where in Jesus' name the devil must bend his knee.

THREE

The Good, the Bad, and the Ugly

You were born to win, but to be a winner, you must plan to win, prepare to win, and expect to win.
—ZIG ZIGLAR

Today's egalitarian world has elevated political correctness to trump truth. It has succeeded in reducing everything to the lowest common denominator lest we offend anyone. The mere thought that not all prayer is good prayer is blasphemy to the PC adherents. Well, in this chapter I want to address the good, the bad, and the ugly issues surrounding prayer because my end goal is for you to experience the fullness of what the Bible promises on answered prayer.

I tell you, you can pray for anything, and if you believe that you've received it, it will be yours. (Mark 11:24 NLT)

Many years ago I felt like I had crossed a line where I no longer simply believed in prayer; I depended upon it. PUSH aims to dispel many of the myths, mistruths, and misunderstandings about prayer while at the same time bringing to light much of what the Bible teaches on effective, powerful prayer.

Authority vs. Power

There is a difference between authority and power. Most people are quick to reach for power. It's instant, impressive, and can cause you to bring about payback on your enemies in a flash! Yes, power is pretty awesome. God wants us to live in power and sends the Holy Spirit upon us for that reason. However, He also wants us to live with authority. Authority seems to be much like the redheaded stepchild of power and is rarely talked about. Yet it is one of the most fundamental and important precepts to establish before we even begin to tackle the subject of how to PUSH in prayer.

Recently I was watching "The World's Strongest Man" competition on ESPN. Let me just say that those guys were freaks! They were blowing up hot water bottles like they were balloons at a kid's birthday party, moving giant boulders, and then came the ultimate event—truck pulling! That's right, one man pulling a giant 18-wheeler truck and trailer. Veins were popping, muscles were bulging, faces were contorting, and groans were wrenching as each man tried to move the truck a distance of ten yards across a white line.

They were massive, with muscles in places I didn't even know existed or have muscles. I certainly wouldn't want to upset these Herculean monsters and possibly find myself on the receiving end of a beating. I'm allergic to drinking steak through a straw in hospitals. Yet as powerful as they were, if I were to put them on the middle of the freeway with a Mack truck hurtling toward them at sixty-five miles per hour and ask them to do their best to stop its forward momentum, at best these giant freaks of nature may make a dent, a muscular brute-shaped impression in the front of the vehicle as it continued down the freeway at sixty-four miles an hour. However, what would you say if I told you I could get a man one-third the size of these hulk-like men and position him on the same freeway with the same Mack truck hurtling toward him and he could stop the truck dead in its tracks without any harm to his person? Intrigued?

Simple. All I need to do is put a police uniform on the smaller man and have him hold a flashing blue light, and the truck would pull to the side of the road and come to a complete halt, without the man even breaking a sweat. Why? Because he possesses authority! He carries the full authority of the government of the land. That's how authority trumps power!

You have authority over the evil one. In Christ you have the power to cast him out, to bind him, to evict him, to command him to leave. PUSH is praying from an elevated position of authority!

However, there is still a very common belief held by believers and unbelievers alike, and that is the blind notion of *fate*. No doubt you have heard people say things like, "Well if it's meant to be, it's meant to be!" The other night I was watching a rugby game that was won in overtime by way of a field goal. During an interview, the captain of the losing team remarked, "Well, I guess it just wasn't meant to be!" Really? Does God decide which teams are going to win games and which ones will lose? Is He betting on this stuff?

Dangerous Paradigms: If It Happens, It Must Be Fate

Even though about 90 percent of Americans believe in a God or a higher power, studies reveal just how wide and varied the beliefs are that people hold about fate, destiny, and the will of God. This is very important for one simple truth: what we believe shapes what we perceive and determines what we ultimately receive.

For example, in the parable of the talents we see this principle in play. Three different men were entrusted with varying sums of money. A talent was about three years of wages. One received one talent, another two, and another five. Yet of the three men there were only two different beliefs about the master. One viewed him as an austere man, the other two as a benevolent, generous man (after all, he gave them all something of value that belonged to him and that they had not earned). The two who believed he was a generous man and a rewarder immediately put the money to work, investing it for a return. But the man who received the one talent buried it, refusing even to place it in the hands of the bankers who manage money day in and day out, who for a fee would make sure that the investment would safely increase and not be lost. Because of what he believed, he was disappointingly unproductive and unfruitful. Upon giving an account to his master, his perception of the master manifested by way of excuse and blame shifting. He scoffed that his master was a man who reaped where he had not sown, and gathered where he had not scattered seed (Matt. 25:24). His perception was formed by his belief about the master, and it ultimately brought about what he received. What do you believe about your heavenly Father, your Master? Do you believe He is an austere master, one who gathers where He does not scatter, one who reaps where He does not sow? Or do you believe Him to be a generous master who benevolently gives us what we don't deserve, affords us great opportunity, and then rewards diligence and fruitfulness greatly? What you believe will determine what you receive.

We see another example of this in Numbers 13. Twelve spies from the children of Israel went to check out the promised land, and ten believed they couldn't take the land because of the size of the men they saw there. They said, "There we saw the giants . . . and we were like grasshoppers in our own sight, and so we were in their sight" (Num. 13:33). This perception kept them from obeying the Lord and crossing over to dispossess the nations that occupied their inheritance. *Belief* shaped what they *perceived*, which in turn shaped what they ultimately *received*. They perished in the wilderness and did not receive the promise God had for them.

Joshua and Caleb, on the other hand, *believed* God had given them the land as an inheritance. They *perceived* that "they are our bread; their protection has departed from them, and the LORD is with us. Do not fear them" (Num. 14:9). And they ultimately *received* the land as an inheritance. Believe, perceive, receive! Three very powerful truths when it comes to inheriting the promises of God. Three very significant truths when it comes to praying effectively. Praying until something happens is about pushing you into a right belief, which in turn will shape your perception, which will result in you receiving all that God has purchased for you through the cross.

What people believe in life affects what they receive in life. If you believe that life is unfair and cruel, then you will find that life will seemingly be stacked against you all your days. If you believe that life is full of opportunity and the world is an endless array of prospects and adventure, life will certainly become a wonderful adventure for you. In the New Testament followers of Jesus Christ were referred to as "believers" for the simple reason that salvation is determined by the act of believing alone.

The infamous scripture finding its way onto TV screens at every Olympic games or major sporting event is John 3:16: "For God so loved the world that He gave His only begotten Son, that whoever *believes* in Him should not perish but have everlasting life" (emphasis added). The truth is every human being is a believer in something. We were created to believe. Faith is not a matter of fact but of belief. Speak with atheists, and they will most likely tell you that they believe in science, that human intellect and technology have replaced any need for belief in God in their lives. Travel to the East, and you will find people who do not eat meat because they believe in reincarnation, that their cow could well be Uncle Joe. And who wants to eat Uncle Joe? Belief is not limited to religious position. We were designed to believe.

When we were children, we believed in Santa Claus bringing presents at Christmas in exchange for 365 days of good behavior, because "He knows when you've been sleeping. He knows when you're awake. He knows if you've been bad or good, so be good for goodness' sake!" What, is the guy eavesdropping? Is he stalking me? Aren't there laws against this kind of thing? But far greater than our belief in Santa, reindeer, Easter bunnies, and the like is what we believe about ourselves (our value and self-worth) and our perception of the world around us.

Being a youth pastor for more than fifteen years, one thing became very obvious: women date their self-esteem! I could not believe over the years how many stunningly beautiful girls would date and end up with absolute losers. It perplexed me so badly. I thought, *Don't they have any mirrors in their homes? Can't they see that they deserve better? What do they see? How do they see themselves?* It's not what we see in the mirror—it's *what* we see in our mirror. If that doesn't make sense and seems like a contradiction, let me explain. Science has proven that we do not see so much *with* the eye as we see *through* it.

This means the young, next top model looking into the mirror may not actually see "America's next top model"; she may see, "You're worthless and of little value, just like your drunk daddy told you! Unless you look like those girls in the magazines you are never going to be loved or beautiful. If that means starving yourself it's worth it." The young man may look in the mirror and not see what God sees—a young man full of gifts, talent, and potential— but instead he sees a shell of a man, full of faults, riddled with insecurity, lacking confidence, and of so little value that his dad left him and the family when he was just a kid. After all, if he was worth more wouldn't Dad have stayed?

What people believe affects the choices they make. There's that old adage, "Our choices affect our habits, which in turn shape our character and determine our destiny." We become the sum total of our choices. What we believe is so important because it affects the choices we make in life, love, and career.

The adult film industry is filled with young girls and women who have been made beautiful on the outside, but on the inside what they believe about themselves is so bankrupt that they allow men who do not love, value, or respect them to sexually abuse and mistreat them. Statistics show that something like 95 percent of these women come from homes where they have suffered some form of abuse.[1]

Young men join gangs, get involved in all kinds of crime, and get hooked on drugs not because they are evil but because they are hungry—hungry for acceptance. There are three A's that are essential to every soul: Acceptance, Affirmation, and Approval. Through the breakdown of the nuclear family, Satan has seen to it that these are in short supply and have become as rare a commodity as fine pearls.

You were created to believe. But *what* you believe is so important. In fact, it is so important that God commissions His followers to go into all the world and preach the gospel (good news) so that whoever would *believe* would not perish.

What do you believe about you? About God? About His plans for your life? Do you believe He is good, bad, indifferent? What do you believe about your potential? At the end of the day, your life will not reflect what you hoped but rather what you believed. That's why I love building the church, the house of God, because it is a *house of belief*! It will help you to believe for God's best to come to pass in your life. Christians are formerly known and called believers. Let me show you how powerful "belief" is!

The twelve spies in Numbers 13 visited the promised land. Ten came back believing a very negative report. However, two spies returned believing a good report that the land could indeed be taken. Who was right, the ten or the two? That's a trick question—all twelve were correct. The ten who said it cannot be done were 100 percent correct; they did not take the land and died in the wilderness. The two who said, "It can be done," were also 100 percent correct; they entered the land, sacked cities, defeated giants, and conquered their mountains.

What Did Jesus Teach?

Jesus understands the principles of God better than anyone else and delivers the following edict when it comes to prayer:

> So Jesus answered and said to them, "Have faith in God. For assuredly, I say to you, whoever says to this mountain, 'Be removed and be cast into the sea,' and does not doubt in his heart, but believes that those things he says will be done, he will have whatever he says. Therefore I say to you, whatever things you ask when you pray, believe that you receive them, and you will have them." (Mark 11:22–24)

Do you see it? Jesus challenges us to *believe* that God is benevolent and good and listening to us when we pray. He challenges us to *perceive* that whatever we ask for, God's power and Word in our lives contain enough power to move mountains, if necessary, to bring it to pass. Our obedience and adherence to this determine what we *receive*. There it is again: *believe, perceive, receive!*

The Power of God Is Limited to Your Belief

Before you label me a heretic, hear me out. It was God's will that all twelve entered into the land and inherited the promise of God for their lives, but what they believed limited what God was able to do in their lives. Jesus died to save the whole world, but it's limited to what people believe. As Henry Ford once said, "Whether you think you can, or you think you can't, you're right!"

I was reading some quotes on my Twitter page and came across the quote of a young person who said, "I don't really care what happens, because if something bad happens it was meant to happen, and you can't change it!" Really? Who told him that?

Many years ago when I worked for an engineering firm in Australia, I became friends with a work colleague who was a little older than me. We shared a common interest in surfing. We had a few surfs together, and the subject of faith and God came up fairly regularly. He always stated emphatically that he was an atheist and did not believe in God, but one day he said that he did believe in fate. I asked him what he meant by "fate." He replied that he believed everything that is meant to happen will happen, and there's nothing we can do about it. So I asked him *who* "meant" it to happen to make it happen? He stammered and could see that his atheism had come to a T-junction. "I guess . . . some sort of . . . um, higher power . . . not saying God . . . maybe aliens . . . but yeah, something. Mother Nature or something!"

About six months later a very kind, jolly gentleman who worked in our department had a heart attack and died over the weekend. A funeral was held a few days later where my friend and I sat beside each other and shared our last respects. All of a sudden my fate-believing friend turned to me and said, "He was such a good bloke. Why did God let this happen? Now you know why I don't believe in God." It's amazing how people who profess that they don't believe in God love to blame Him whenever something bad happens. What happened to fate? "It was meant to be," wasn't it? Would it shock you if I told you that fate is a very present belief system even among many who profess to be Christians? This belief is based on the presupposition that God has set everything in motion like some giant windup clock and then has stepped back, waiting for the alarm to ring to signal the end of the age.

A lot of deists believe that God is no longer involved or even interested in human affairs. Like the nineteenth-century philosopher Friedrich Nietzsche, they herald that "God is dead." Or like some scientists proclaimed in the 1980s, "God is dead. We believe He died in the 1500s."[2]

Many people believe that we are powerless, like tiny ants trying unsuccessfully to stop a runaway freight train.

Fatalists believe that we are like children strapped into the backseat of a car hurtling along the freeway at breakneck speed, dangerously drifting across the lanes toward disaster because the driver is slumped over the wheel, dead from a heart attack. We can scream all we want—God cannot and will not do anything to save us.

Fatalist Christians Become Apathetic Christians

In the 2012 US presidential election, the incumbent president Barack Obama was running against the Republican nominee Mitt Romney. Pretty much all of the pundits believed that Romney was going to win based on the fact that no president in history who had allowed unemployment to rise to double digits had ever been reelected. The economy was a mess, the Bush-blaming rhetoric was beginning to wear thin on both sides of the political fence, and the debt had increased more in the first term of President Obama than in all eight years of the previous president.

But as we know, Obama won reelection, and Romney faded into oblivion. What was sad was that many evangelical Christians didn't even bother to vote. The ticket had become quite divided. Obama, having zero credibility to run on his record of leadership, began to reach out to the extreme factions of the liberal left: gay marriage, legalization of marijuana, on-demand abortion funded by the taxpayer, global warming purveyors, and the like. All of these things are pretty much opposed by the evangelical Christian belief. Yet very few Christians turned out to vote. Pulpits were deafeningly quiet with pastors not wanting to risk upsetting folks in their churches in order to keep their budgets and lifestyles intact.

The most common statement I heard after the election was,

"Well, it's whoever God wanted it to be!" Really? Voting is a pointless exercise? People were walking around saying, "Whoever God wanted to win won!" Really? So when Hitler won election in the 1930s, that was God's choice? Pol Pot, Mao Zedong, Kim Jong Il, and Saddam Hussein were all whom God wanted? Last time I looked, the Bible teaches that our choices carry consequences, and therefore we ought not to consider appointing leadership as a light thing. Especially when fiscal responsibility, sanctity of life, and Judeo-Christian morality had received shattering blows under President Obama.

When people say things like, "Yeah, it's not for us to worry about our nation. Whoever God wants to rule will rule anyway," once again it is fatalism saying that your vote, your will, and your efforts are incidental and have no effect because what God wants comes to pass whether we like it or not. That is not consistent with what we see in the opening pages of the Bible in Genesis. In fact, we see the exact opposite. Man chose to eat from the tree that was forbidden even though God had warned him and commanded him not to!

Are we to believe, then, that *every* ruler is appointed by God, despite the desire and will of the people? People like Iran's president Ahmadinejad who had 30,000 protestors gunned down? "It's okay, whoever God wants to rule will rule!" If you take this line of reasoning a little farther, then you have to deduce that if God does indeed choose *every* leader, the atrocities committed by these tyrants (approaching a hundred million lives brutally wiped out) must be accredited to God, who chose them to lead in the first place.

When a nation turns its back on God, it *alone* chooses, by the exercise of its free will, which leaders it wants to rule over it. Consequently these leaders who have no belief in or desire to adhere to God's will become destructive dictators and greatly damage their nation. Proverbs says it well: "When the righteous are in authority, the people rejoice; but when a wicked man rules, the people groan" (29:2).

Fate and Evil

If everything that happens is God's will or has been predetermined by fate, then we remove a very cogent fact from the equation: evil is a tangible reality in our universe, and evil has a will that seeks to effect, influence, and cause certain outcomes! To put it another way, not only does evil exist, but it is actually driven by a highly intelligent personality presiding over a complex hierarchical system. This evil kingdom carries a strong vision to continually oppose and resist the will of God from coming to pass on the earth. God is not the author of evil. God does not cause evil. At best He allows certain things to take place, but to say He causes it is to misunderstand the character of God.

Pop Culture Shapes Our World

Satan knows how powerful the Word of God is because it shapes and frames the world in which we live. God spoke "Let there be light" (Gen. 1:3), and light was. Adam was to rule and govern by the words of his mouth. Our words can bring hope or they can invoke fear and hopelessness. An entire generation forfeited their entry into the promised land because of words that assassinated hope in their hearts.

Recent Supreme Court decisions have succeeded in removing the Bible from places like schools and higher-education establishments and the Ten Commandments from our courthouses. This has resulted in a vacuum where the enemy is eagerly able to substitute the Word of God (truth) with lies (false words). We are governed by words. They are used to establish legislation, create contracts, fuel hope, shape lives, and inspire sports teams to leave nothing on the field when that final whistle blows. Words shape. Satan has made sure that our world is filled with darkness by removing the Word of God (which produces light) and replacing it with words of wickedness, hopelessness, fear, perversion, and deceit. Why not? It worked in Eden: "Has God really said . . . ?" was his solicitation.

Our current pop-culture-obsessed generation bows in homage to the prophets and prophetesses who carry these words, putting them to song, sound, and screen. Hypnotized fans worship their pied pipers. Meanwhile a generation is proselytized into adopting the mantra of this new world religion, decreeing that "fame equals success."

Many of these young child stars in the news media face criminal charges for all kinds of misdemeanors. Some end up in rehab suffering from various types of addictions, the fallout of this indulgent lifestyle. Others sadly are simply discarded like last year's iPhone to make way for the next child-star sensation to rise up and take their place. Worse still, some end up in the local morgue. Yet the appetite is whetted, and the lust for fame demands new stars and starlets. Networks eager to profit readily supply more of this drug as we continue to sacrifice our emerging generation to Molech (the Canaanite god of fame, success, and power). What is shaping your worldview, the Word of God or the words of this age? One may be louder than the other, but never sacrifice volume for validity!

Pop Culture Carries a Message

Doris Day famously sang a song called "Que Sera, Sera," which translated means, "Whatever will be, will be." The entire song is about the future not being ours to see, so why bother with it. Whatever is meant to happen is going to happen. You can't control it. It's already predetermined. Yet our culture today is more obsessed with palm readers, psychics, mediums, and spiritualists than ever before.

"The future's not ours to see." Really? That's not what the Bible teaches. Look at these verses: "And it shall come to pass afterward that I will pour out My Spirit on all flesh; your sons and your daughters shall prophesy, your old men shall dream dreams, your young men shall see visions" (Joel 2:28). Prophesying, dreams, and visions *all have to do with the future.*

The outcome of our progressive, secular, post-Christian culture is a melting pot of superstitious beliefs. Everything from the alignment of the planets, star signs, and crystals, to certain rocks apparently are influencing fortune and destiny. It seems that the Enlightenment movement has only succeeded in burying people in darkness. With new "God-removing" fads, such as *The Secret*, emerging every three to seven years, we see a secular society trying to snap up biblical principles while simultaneously removing the author of these principles from any credit or involvement. According to *The Secret*, we simply ask the "universe" for what we want in life and then believe that the universe hears us and responds accordingly! Those who are "too intelligent for God" gobble this up with wanton abandon. What's next, leprechauns and pixies, pots of gold at the end of the rainbow?

This theme dominates popular culture today—do not think that Doris Day is the only one to embrace this theme. So do bands like Oasis, Nirvana, Coldplay, and even ABBA. Yes, the former super-Swede sensations also have hopelessness and fatalism as pervasive beliefs throughout the lyrics of their songs. One in particular is the song "The Winner Takes It All," a massive hit for the Swedish fab four that documents the pain of band members' marriages breaking under the weight of fame and stardom. The song speaks specifically about the pain of divorce, declaring that there are winners and there are losers, with the "winner" taking it all. And "the gods may throw the dice . . . and someone way down here loses someone dear."[3] Wow, it seems fate is in the hands of the gods, and these gods are completely uncaring and indifferent to the desires, affections, and needs of our human plight.

This idea was certainly popular throughout both the Roman and Grecian dynasties, evidenced by the plethora of gods that were worshiped by those empires. The gods required constant appeasement so that one might somehow attain some level of success in life's pursuits of love, life, family, health, and prosperity. To upset the gods in any way meant certain calamity, misery, and misfortune.

This fatalistic, hopeless belief makes continual resurgences in every generational cycle. Perhaps it is because on a surface level it answers the much-asked enigma of "why do bad things happen to good people?" The answer it provides is that there are forces or gods beyond our control who influence luck and providence in our lives on this planet. A rabbit's foot, or touching wood, or a four-leaf clover purchases some much-needed relief from these forces/ gods and also gets you favor. But you cannot count on them; they are unpredictable, capricious, and temperamental, given to whims and tantrums. And when it comes to our needs, they really don't care at all. Life is reduced to nothing more than a matter of luck and fate.

Thank God for the gift of prayer. Your life and your fate are not already decided, but have been placed into your hands: "Whatever you bind on earth will be bound in heaven, and whatever you loose on earth will be loosed in heaven" (Matt. 16:19). In other words, the ball is in your court as to the kind of life you are going to live here on earth! You have been given a divine blessing to be an heir of the great power of heaven, so that you are not at the mercy of life's storms and circumstances but can actually exercise authority over them. Didn't you ever wonder why Jesus rebuked the disciples in the boat in Mark 4 when they were sailing across the Sea of Galilee to the land of the Gadarenes? A giant windstorm arose, and Jesus was asleep on a pillow. The disciples woke Him not because they believed He had power over the wind and the elements, but because He seemed so calm in the midst of what was a very, very serious situation. They were in jeopardy, according to the gospel of Luke, and there was Jesus just snoozing away.

Jesus stood and rebuked the wind and the waves, saying, "Peace, be still" (Mark 4:39). Then He rebuked the disciples for their lack of faith. Not because He was a grumpyhead and woke up on the wrong side of the boat, but because the storm was not immovable. They were not at the mercy of the wind and waves, but as children of God had been given authority and dominion over the whole earth. But authority is of little benefit if it is not exercised. Jesus said, "Whatever you ask in My name, that will I do, that the Father may be glorified in the Son. If you ask anything in My name, I will do it" (John 14:13–14).

What are you asking for? And if you are asking, are you believing? Too often we disqualify ourselves with thoughts like, *I'm not good enough to ask for that. God has much more deserving, holier people than me. Who am I to pray?*

My kids are my kids no matter what grades they turn in at school. Obviously I reward and bless them when they make an A because I know it's hard work and something worth celebrating. However, when they get an F, I don't say, "Well, you gotta find somewhere else to sleep tonight, and don't even ask if I am feeding you dinner. You are no longer my child!" Child protective services would be called, and I would be deemed unfit to parent. So why do we think our heavenly Father is like that? He loves you and is for you and hears you when you pray based not upon your performance, but rather upon His victory at Calvary!

The Dark Ages

There was a time in history known as the Dark Ages, when superstition reigned supreme and life was filled with tyrannical dictatorships, corruption in religion, and witch hunts resulting in various forms of human suffering. What was the underlying cause of the Dark Ages? It was the removal of public access to light and truth—the Bible being removed from society.

Jesus said, "I am the light of the world. He who follows Me shall not walk in darkness, but have the light of life" (John 8:12). He was declaring that we would live free from fear and superstition when we walk with Him, but be dominated by it without Him. Jesus is the Word of God (John 1:1). David declared, "Your word is a lamp to my feet and a light to my path" (Ps. 119:105).

Not content to simply remove the Bible from public access, the clergy of the day decided to translate it into Latin, the language of the educated and upper class. This meant that only the clergy and the wealthy aristocrats could read it and explain it to the commoner, providing incredible leverage to control and manipulate the masses as they desired for personal gain.

If people could read the Scriptures for themselves, they would realize that they did not need the priests' approval to have their sins forgiven; they could go directly to Jesus Christ themselves, and therefore live without fear of hell and damnation, but have assurance of eternal life. But when man wants to take power underhandedly, all kinds of corruption and moral degradation ensue. Thousands of innocent people died through witch hunts and other evils directly attributed to the superstitions that prevailed in the vacuum of truth created by the removal of the Word of God.

Your life is *not* in the hands of capricious gods. Neither is it dependent upon the universe, cosmic energy, innate intelligence, crystals, planetary alignment, your birthday, star signs, and other forces beyond your control all somehow being favorable toward you. Your life is *not* in the hands of fate. The following verse is one of my favorite verses in all of Scripture because it challenges the very concept of fate. In doing so, it removes the most destructive side effect of fate—being rendered a "powerless victim," nothing more than a bystander in the play of life, reduced to a spectator in the theater of the living: "I returned and saw under the sun that—the race is not to the swift, nor the battle to the strong, nor bread to the wise, nor riches to men of understanding, nor favor to men of skill; but time and chance happen to them all" (Eccl. 9:11). In other words, God gives *all* of us time and chance, the ability to seize opportunities and create our own future and fortune.

You and I were created with the power to reason, to believe, to dream, to envision, to imagine, to create, and to choose. These are not only the gifts of God—these are the attributes of God. Alfred, Lord Tennyson once said, "For man is man and master of his fate!"[4] You were created to master. God gave mankind power and dominion.

Nowhere in the Scriptures did Jesus teach that if something was meant to happen that it would, or that we as mere human beings are neutered, excluded, and left impotent to do anything to prevent or change it. In fact, Jesus both taught and modeled the exact opposite. Jesus said, "Unless you repent you will all likewise perish" (Luke 13:3). In other words, your choices and belief systems determine your destiny. Jesus said "Have faith in God" and "All things are possible to him who believes" (Mark 11:22; Mark 9:23). Both of these scriptures were in the context of seeing the power of God work for you to change circumstances.

Choice Is the Exercise of Will

When Jesus prayed in the Garden of Gethsemane, He cried out to God His Father, saying, "Father, all things are possible for You. Take this cup away from Me; nevertheless, not what I will, but what You will" (Mark 14:36). Jesus' prayer reveals that the gap between God's perfect will and our own will is the presence of choice. Choice is the gift afforded us when God gave us free will. When our free will lines up with God's will, we choose His way over ours. This is called devotion, worship, faithfulness, love, and loyalty, and this is when powerful things begin to happen in and through our lives!

Judgment Is the Price of Free Will

Choice may certainly be the exercise of free will, but judgment is the *price* of free will. There can be no free will without judgment. Whether we realize it or not, each and every decision we make is weighed by judgment. The decision to purchase a new automobile, the decision to put your kids into a private school, the choice to go skydiving—every decision we make is weighed against the collective wisdom of our peers, loved ones, and if you're in the public service, by complete strangers and critics. Opinions are passed and discussed adjudicating whether the choice you made was wise or foolish, beneficial or futile, vain or selfless. This is why in Ecclesiastes the author makes the declaration: "Rejoice, O young man, in your youth, and let your heart cheer you in the days of your youth; walk in the ways of your heart, and in the sight of your eyes; but know that for all these God will bring you into judgment" (11:9).

It is this judgment that keeps men accountable. My choices carry consequences, and there is a loving, holy God whom I must stand before and give an account to. What makes a man wicked and corrupts and destroys societies is the myth or lie that there is no God and therefore no judgment or accountability. Look at what the Scripture teaches in Psalm 10:13: "Why do the wicked renounce God? He has said in his heart, 'You will not require an account.'"

We all have a free will to choose, but our choices carry consequences. Some say, "Well then, I'm not really free at all, because if I don't choose God I'm condemned." The truth is God has given us His laws for our benefit and protection. God exists, and so do His moral laws. Gravity exists whether it's convenient or not. It is not limiting my free will when I choose to jump out of an airplane; it just reinforces the fact that gravity is a reality and my choice to have a parachute or not will have either a pleasant or dire outcome.

"I Like Fate Because Then I'm Not Responsible"

It *amazes* me how so many Christians inadvertently have "fate" underlying their theology but label it as "the sovereignty of God." I was in a meeting recently attempting to purchase some real estate. A Christian group had purchased a certain property at the peak of the market in the hopes of developing it and using it for the glory of God. When circumstances changed, they were struck with the realization that they, too, had overreached, and it would no longer be financially equitable for them to develop the property further without jeopardizing their resources and other projects they had in play. So they decided to sell the property.

The problem was their asking price was almost 40 percent above the current market value, and their logic was based upon a hope that God would do a miracle and bail them out of their poor business decision. Upon counsel from experts in the real estate business to drop the price of the property to something realistic, the group confessed that a parishioner had put in more than 50 percent of the purchase price as a cash loan, which was to be paid back upon the sale of the property or upon refinancing. They needed it to be sold at an above market price to save their skin. The project was already hemorrhaging hundreds of thousands of dollars per month, so time was certainly working against them. When a fair offer finally came in, they would not even consider it. Despite all the counsel from their broker and other leaders, the thought of selling at a massive financial loss, licking their wounds, and putting it down to education was anathema.

"We just trust God knows what He is doing!" was the

group's response. I was flabbergasted. I couldn't help but imagine God in heaven saying, *Umm, I am the God of wisdom, and I give to all men liberally. All you have to do is ask me or consult me before you purchase. I may see a thing or two that you do not see. But you were too blinded by gain and opportunity, and you saw "good," not "God," in this transaction. And now all of a sudden it's my issue? Really?*

This may come as a shock, but the Bible teaches that there are consequences to each and every action, choice, purchase, and decision we make. So Scripture behooves us to seek His face, wisdom, and counsel. Jesus was the personification of faith and yet gave this wise instruction:

> For which of you, intending to build a tower, does not sit down first and count the cost, whether he has enough to finish it— lest, after he has laid the foundation, and is not able to finish, all who see it begin to mock him, saying, "This man began to build and was not able to finish"? Or what king, going to make war against another king, does not sit down first and consider whether he is able with ten thousand to meet him who comes against him with twenty thousand? Or else, while the other is still a great way off, he sends a delegation and asks conditions of peace. (Luke 14:28–32)

The businessmen's theology was rooted in a fatalistic perception of God's sovereignty. That goes something along the lines of, "If I wasn't meant to do it, then I wouldn't be able to do it; therefore it must be God's will." This does not line up with sound doctrine taught anywhere in the Scriptures, but rather is contrary to the teachings of the Bible. You can choose wrongly; God will allow it because He has designated a day when we will all give an account for these choices.

Perhaps God Is Drunk?

I recently read a letter a pastor sent to his congregants asking them to please pray for, think of, and bless the staff he had to let go because the giving had gone down in the church due to the GFC (Global Financial Crisis) and consequential downturn of the economy. The letter attempted to garner some sympathy and maybe conjure up a little guilt for people backing off from their giving. Again, what struck me was the statement, "We are just trusting the Lord knows what He is doing!" Is God some type of aimless drunk behind the wheel of a car?

The thinking at play here is the belief that our choices are inconsequential to the will of God. Everything that happens is God's will—the economic downturn and the lack of finances in the church. It couldn't possibly be man's fault, could it? Could it be that the church offerings are low because the pastor has failed to put faith in his people in the midst of an economic famine? Could it be that the church has not exercised wisdom in its management of cash-flow and income/expense management? There is a paradigm I have come across that God should just automatically bail us out (like the government did with GM) whenever we misspend or fail to steward our resources wisely. Now while I absolutely believe God is gracious and abundant in mercy, He is also righteous and just and has set principles in play that benefit us when applied but have dire consequences when ignored. It's like the guy who eats every meal at McDonald's, supersizes everything, and then a few months later wonders why God does not fix his ailing health.

The danger of this kind of thinking is a presupposition that the sovereignty of God abdicates us from responsibility for our choices. That everything that goes well does so because it *must* have been God's will. In other words, they would not have been able to purchase the land in the first place *unless* it was God's will. The error of this thinking is such that they believe that *nothing* happens apart from God's will. A successful bank heist therefore *must* have been God's will. A prosperous kidnapping venture— God's will! Or could it be that there are things that are successful without God's involvement at all? If you say, "No, if something is successful God *must* have been in on it!" then I must point out that you are wrong. The Bible tells us so in Genesis 11. The Tower of Babel was *not* the will of God—it was the will of man—and God saw that they were having success independent of His involvement. But that's another chapter.

Fate has people believing that free will is an illusion, that in actuality your every decision has already been pre-made for you by a force or forces outside of your control. Forget "the devil made me do it!" Just say, "I'm not responsible. God programmed me to do it—everything that happens is God's will!" That's not going to work, I'm afraid. You are responsible whether you like it or not.

Choices, Actions, Consequences

Do not believe that *whatever* God wants or wills will just automatically happen or that we are incidental players in a giant cosmic game of chess with our moves completely overridden by God, the giant chess master in the sky. The Bible teaches the exact opposite of this. God's will was for Moses to take the children of Israel across the Jordan into the promised land. However, Moses' disobedience at the rock caused God to grieve and Moses to miss out on entry into the land of Canaan. Saul had first dibs on being king of Israel, but his constant disobedience and self-seeking caused the kingdom to be torn from him.

The Bible teaches us in 1 Corinthians that a whole generation perished in the wilderness because of their actions and God not being pleased with them. Their story was written for our admonition.

Moreover, brethren, I do not want you to be unaware that all our fathers were under the cloud, all passed through the sea, all were baptized into Moses in the cloud and in the sea, all ate the same spiritual food, and all drank the same spiritual drink. For they drank of that spiritual Rock that followed them, and that Rock was Christ. But with most of them God was not well pleased, for their bodies were scattered in the wilderness.

Now these things became our examples, to the intent that we should not lust after evil things as they also lusted. And do not become idolaters as were some of them. As it is written, "The people sat down to eat and drink, and rose up to play." Nor let us commit sexual immorality, as some of them did, and in one day twenty-three thousand fell; nor let us tempt Christ, as some of them also tempted, and were destroyed by serpents; nor complain, as some of them also complained, and were destroyed by the destroyer. Now all these things happened to them as examples, and they were written for our admonition, upon whom the ends of the ages have come. (1 Cor. 10:1–11)

This may come as a shock, but *our actions carry consequences*! We may not like to read that, but it's true. Some say things like, "My life is a mess; I just hope God knows what He is doing." Yeah, He does, but when we ignore the counsel of His Word we usually end up in disappointment, loss, and pain. We don't succeed so much in breaking God's laws as we succeed in breaking ourselves against them. This relates to marriage, family, finances, business, and life in general. God's Word has wisdom for life and success. God's edict to Joshua, the successor of Moses, was for him to meditate on God's law day and night and not let it depart from his mouth, for then he would make his way prosperous and have good success (Josh. 1:8). God's Word brings life, success, and prosperity in every area of our lives. When we ignore it, we do so to our peril.

I heard a person lament, "We just don't know why God is doing this to us; we don't know what He is trying to teach us," after co-starting a company that had all the symptoms of a get-rich-quick scheme. Despite counsel to the contrary, new cars were purchased as well as a new home in a very expensive community, and credit cards were maxed out as the money would soon come pouring in.

Some think that giving their business a Christian name or saying "this business is for God" substitutes for hard work, wisdom, and diligence. God should bless it with success simply because it is "for" Him. Unfortunately, the marketplace does not operate like this. *Luck favors the prepared* in the marketplace. There is no fast track to success beyond working hard and working smart.

Calling the pastor and asking him for some clarity as to why the "big bail-out dude" in the sky is not kicking into gear is the go-to for too many folks. The philosophy being we make our own choices and decisions independent of God and His counsel, yet if these decisions could hurt us then He ought to jump into gear and prevent our pain. God does *not* punish us for our foolish decisions; our foolish decisions suffice in doing that all by themselves. As I have heard preached many times, "We are not punished for our sins so much as we are punished *by* our sins."

Even Satan tried to fool Jesus with a perversion of Scripture:

> Then he brought Him to Jerusalem, set Him on the pinnacle of the temple, and said to Him, "If You are the Son of God, throw Yourself down from here. For it is written: 'He shall give His angels charge over you, to keep you,' and, 'In their hands they shall bear you up, lest you dash your foot against a stone.'" And Jesus answered and said to him, "It has been said, 'You shall not tempt the LORD your God.'" (Luke 4:9–12)

The devil was trying to deceive Jesus into believing the very same lie, that somehow His choices had no consequence or effect upon the will of God for His life. He could throw Himself down in an apparent "suicide attempt" or engage in actions of self-harm, but He would be invincible and immortal because God had ordained for angels to protect Him. However, Jesus responded by declaring that our choices should work *with* the will of God for our lives, not *against* the will of God for our lives. All choices have consequences. God gave us the power to choose our own way. That's why it is imperative that we live being led by the Spirit and walk in the counsel of the Word of God. Two great places to start!

FOUR

The Fight Club

Prayer does not change the purpose of God.
But prayer does change the action of God.
—CHUCK SMITH

Prayer is a battle. Sometimes it may not feel like it; other times it is all battle and little joy. The soul delights in prayer. It is how it breathes. The spirit is invigorated through prayer. It is how it gets recharged. The flesh . . . well, it's not too keen on prayer at the best of times. Prayer interrupts its lusts and agenda, putting the things of God ahead of the things of self. The flesh behaves like a small child wanting candy in the checkout line at the grocery store, throwing a tantrum when it's told no. The child doesn't like to hear no, and neither does the flesh. So the first battle of prayer is within us. It becomes a discipline. The dividends of persevering and building to a disciplined prayer life will outweigh almost every other endeavor.

"This charge I commit to you, son Timothy, according to the prophecies previously made concerning you, that by them you may wage the good warfare" (1 Tim.1:18).

Prayer is primarily about conflict. There are two dimensions operating simultaneously, with each seeking to dominate the other. Paul in the above verse beckons Timothy to war in prayer to have his life line up with the prophetic words of God spoken over his life. Even though these words are the words of God, Paul is reminding Timothy that the Word of God and His will inherent within it do not happen automatically but must be pushed into the place of dominion by our engagement of prayer.

There is a constant battle going on over our heads in the spiritual realm. It is in conflict with angels and demons battling over the souls of mankind. We read words like *strongholds* in the Bible. Strongholds are always associated with warfare. The enemy has "built places of fortified resistance" (the Oxford dictionary definition of *stronghold*) in the earth to resist the will of God.

If we were honest, the battle and conflict are not limited to above our heads but rage within our heads and our hearts also. I used to love the old Donald Duck Disney cartoons where Donald is in a conflict and has a small angel Donald sitting on his right shoulder, but a small devil Donald sitting on his left. One is telling him to do what is right, while the other is telling him to do wrong. Whichever one he obeys determines what happens next in his life. I think Walt Disney captured this truth perfectly.

Battle on a Global and Cosmic Scale

The Bible says in the book of Joshua that after the death of Moses, God spoke to Joshua and told him to cross over the Jordan and walk through the land of Canaan and that all the places the soles of his feet shall tread was his divine portion and inheritance. Walking on the ground has to do with dominion. Moses is instructed to take the sandals off his feet because the place where he was standing was "holy ground," literally "belonging to God," and he needed to acknowledge and reverence this fact. When Joshua came to face the fortified stronghold called Jericho, God commanded him to *walk* around it. This is warfare. Now look at this scripture in the book of Job:

> Now there was a day when the sons of God came to present themselves before the LORD, and Satan also came among them. And the LORD said to Satan, "From where do you come?" So Satan answered the LORD and said, "From going to and fro on the earth, and from walking back and forth on it." (1:6–7)

Satan tells God he has come from the earth, that this is his dwelling place. But look at what activity the devil is engaging in. He is *walking back and forth, to and fro, on it!*

Satan is doing this to claim the territory as his own. He has sought a place where his will is done, where he sits on his throne, where he rules. We are caught in the middle of this battle. Whether we like it or not, we are involved in a cosmic conflict and there are eternal consequences at stake. Prayer battles by pushing back the agenda of darkness to establish the kingdom of light. This is the purpose and focus of prayer.

Nothing Comes Easily

I wish I could tell you that everything has come easily for us. But the opposite is true. I wish I could tell you that once you begin to follow Jesus Christ and make Him Lord and Savior of your life, from then on everything becomes easy and peaceful and just falls into place without any effort. The opposite is true.

We moved to San Diego in the summer of 2005, sent by our pastor in Australia, Dr. Phil Pringle, with the sole purpose of starting a city-influencing church here in beautiful Southern California. We began as five people (me, my wife and three sons), and in eight years have grown to almost three thousand people gathering in our weekend services. Some look at this and say, "Wow, God has really blessed you," and He most definitely has. But I must tell you that nothing has come easily. I have felt like we had to fight and PUSH each and every step of the way. It has seemed like we had to fight for each and every individual that has come to be part of our church. It has seemed at times that we have lost more battles than we have won. But still we persist. As the apostle Paul said when he was strengthening and encouraging the church, "We must through many tribulations enter the kingdom of God" (Acts 14:22).

The battle is not won on the sidelines. It is won on the field. Each one of us is called to take the field and establish the kingdom. This only happens through PUSH kind of prayer. It must be forceful, focused, and effective prayer. We push to see the kingdom come first in our own hearts and lives. Then it flows into our families, our communities, and throughout the world in which we live. Because the kingdom of darkness really exists, spiritual warfare will be encountered. But fear not, for "greater is He who is in you than he who is in the world" (1 John 4:4 NASB).

Prayer is the weaponry we have been given to push back the powers of darkness and thwart their wicked agenda. Through the medium of prayer we are able to rise triumphantly in each and every circumstance: "Now thanks be to God who always leads us in triumph in Christ, and through us diffuses the fragrance of His knowledge in every place" (2 Cor. 2:14).

Many would prefer to believe that prayer is nice but not necessary, much like sequins on a motorcycle helmet. So many see prayer as a nonchalant activity rather than powerful productivity, as incidental as opposed to intentional, kind of an "In case of emergency break glass" approach when it comes to prayer. Yet Jesus "often withdrew into the wilderness and prayed" (Luke 5:16). It is the *only* thing the Bible mentions Jesus doing "often." With just three years of public ministry from His launch to His crucifixion, the clock was ticking, and He didn't have a whole lot of free time to kill. He prayed in solitary places often because it was the most productive activity for Him to engage in, fueling and clarifying all that He did.

Too many believe that God's will automatically happens without the medium of prayer. Yet the Bible illustrates that this is not the case. In the gospel of Mark, Jesus is confronted by a leper with a desperate request. "If You are willing, You can make me clean" (Mark 1:40). Jesus then stretches out His hand and says, "I am willing; be cleansed" and immediately the man was healed from leprosy (1:41). If you take the time to look closely at this incident you will discover some helpful truths. First, Jesus said that He was willing, and yet just the fact that it was Jesus' will did not change the condition of the man. It was only when Jesus reached out and touched the man and *spoke* "Be cleansed" that the man was healed. The will of God flows from the proclamation of His Word. When we connect God to a leprous world and speak the Word of God, His will flows, and the leprosy of our human condition leaves!

PUSH Prayer Prays From . . .

We actually pray *from* a place of victory, not *toward* a place of victory!

"From the days of John the Baptist until now the kingdom of heaven suffers violence, and the violent take it by force" (Matt. 11:12). I love that scripture for so many reasons. The New American Standard version says that "violent men" lay hold of it. The word in the original Greek for *violent* here is the word *biaste*, which literally means "a violent man." The word *suffers* is the Greek word *biazo*, which means "to force." They are related words. It literally means that the kingdom advances upon the shoulders of men who are aggressive, not passive—people who push rather than passively accept less than their perceived God's best. These people are not ignorant of God's will, they are not happy to receive anything and everything that comes their way, and they want to lay hold of the kingdom of heaven and *only* what comes from there.

Hosea 4:6 says, "My people are destroyed for lack of knowledge," meaning that ignorance is not bliss—it is destructive, limiting, and damaging. You must know what is unacceptable before you can resist settling for it. Sadly so many people accept far less than God's best; in fact, they accept what the devil has dished out, believing that maybe it comes from God.

Don't settle on the wrong side of the Jordan like two and a half tribes did. Reuben, Gad, and the half tribe of Manasseh were content to settle for less than God's best.

Don't be someone who lives for what is easier—live for what is right! Live for what God has said in His Word, not what seems good or expedient to you. Reuben, Gad, and the half tribe of Manasseh lived in constant struggle from that day forward. They did not want to push one last time across the Jordan and into the land of Canaan. It required a whole lot less effort to simply remain on the east of the Jordan, close to God's promise but not *inside* of God's promised land and God's protection.

A Toxic Culture

We are too busy to pray, and so we are too busy to have power. We have a great deal of activity, but we accomplish little; many services but few conversions; much machinery but few results.
—R. A. TORREY

Christianity has very much Westernized during the last few hundred years and has developed a somewhat dysmorphic perception of war and battle that is not consistent with the teachings of the Bible. Our very anti-war culture believes that peace can be obtained without the use of force or the exercise of authority. If we could just gather enough beauty pageant finalists to declare their devotion to "world peace" and enough Prius drivers to bear bumper stickers stating "Coexist" and "War Is Not the Answer," then surely we could have a world without war. But back in reality, life teaches us that bullies don't quit their bullying antics for your lunch money simply by you giving them all your money before school begins. It requires an intervention of authority and justice to rein in the antics of the bullies and neutralize their negative influence.

Jesus describes the devil as a thief who comes to steal, kill, and destroy (John 10:10). Amazingly, many twenty-first-century believers think Jesus was using hyperbole here to describe Satan and his agenda. But Jesus is not given to exaggeration or lies, as He is the personification of truth. He is describing for us perfectly the character of Satan, who is described by the apostle Peter as an adversary (one who actively opposes) in 1 Peter 5:8. Left unchecked, he will break into your world to steal, plunder, kill, and destroy all the things God has brought into and blessed your life with. He *must* be resisted. He must be pushed out!

The Battle for Connection

The greatest battle you will face in this life is connection with God. Jesus had to leave the crying of the crowd, the demands of the multitude, and the solace of His companions in order to keep His connection with God the Father strong. Prayer is the greatest gift extended to us from heaven because it is direct access to and complete fellowship with God, the Creator of the universe.

Your flesh does not like prayer because it is not used to prayer. You have fed your flesh and its desires from the time you were a nursing infant, so a spiritual appetite must be something that is developed.

You will never find so many distractions as when you set aside time to pray. But you must battle daily for connection—this is how we get our daily bread from heaven. Remember, man does not live by bread alone but by every word that proceeds from the mouth of God (Deut. 8:3). Prayer is accessing the limitless wisdom of God; prayer is an invading of the impossible; and prayer is the way your spirit recharges, confidence and courage replenish, and vitality is restored to your soul. Fight the fight to get connected. It's worth it!

PUSH Is a Stargate, a Portal into Another Dimension

We have already established that God's will *must* intersect with our will before it is able to flow into and through our lives. This intersection happens through prayer.

> Then Abram moved his tent, and went and dwelt by the terebinth trees of Mamre, which are in Hebron, and built an altar there to the LORD. . . . Then the LORD appeared to him by the terebinth trees of Mamre, as he was sitting in the tent door in the heat of the day. (Gen. 13:18; 18:1)

Do you ever wish God would visit you? That God would speak to you, or deliver on His promises to you? Well the above two passages of Scripture show Abraham in two phases of his life. The first one is where he separates from his nephew Lot. Abraham, or Abram (exalted father), was asked by the Lord to leave his father's house, get away from his family, and get out of his country. And like we all do, Abram obeys with some compromise. He takes his nephew Lot with him. What part of "family" did he not understand? Anyway, I believe he took Lot because Lot was his deceased brother's son, and Abram was able to justify this decision a couple of ways. First, Lot needed a father, and Abram was his dad's brother, so Abram would be the best surrogate for him. Second, when people asked him what his name was and he replied Abram—"exalted father"—they would possibly see Lot as his son, and this would help him save face and not have to endure the disappointment and shame of not being able to have children and appearing to be cursed by God. It was just easier to pass off Lot as his own son.

But strife prevails as the dominant culture in the relationship between himself and Lot, as is always the fruit of compromising our obedience to God. Compromise never produces peace, but instead expels it. So Abram realizes his transgression and brings himself to ask Lot to depart for the sake of their relationship. Lot lifts up his eyes and sees the well-watered plains of Canaan toward Sodom and pitches his tent there. Abram goes in the opposite direction, toward a mountainous, arid, far less-appealing terrain and plants his tent by the terebinth trees in Mamre, and there he builds an altar to the Lord. The contrast is striking—Abraham will inherit all he sees, and Lot will lose everything because of all he sees.

What you pitch your tent toward determines your lot in

life—ask Lot. Abraham was in Mamre, meaning "place of vision," and it was there that some twenty years later God appeared to him (Gen. 18:1) and proclaimed that the next year his eighty-nine-year-old wife would bring forth a son from her own body—an incomprehensible miracle for a man who was just about to celebrate his centennial! But with God nothing is impossible. God visited Abraham in the place that Abraham had built for Him. God saved Noah in the place Noah had built for Him. God visited Israel with fire in the place Elijah had built for Him.

PUSH prayer is a portal, a stargate into a realm where all things are possible. It's a place where the goodness of God overcomes the wickedness of the world, where God's perfect will in heaven can manifest here on earth in our lives.

Heavenly Wars

And war broke out in heaven: Michael and his angels fought with the dragon; and the dragon and his angels fought, but they did not prevail, nor was a place found for them in heaven any longer. (Rev. 12:7–8)

It's very interesting where the first war in history took place. It was not on the earth. It was in heaven. This is a tough pill to swallow for those who believe everything that happens is the will of God. In fact, the reason behind the war was a conflict of wills. Satan, the dragon, was in rebellion, deciding that his will would be done, not God's will! Isn't the source of all conflict, war, strife, and disappointment in our lives traced back to a moment when our hearts decided, "My will be done and not *Thy* will"?

Make no mistake, the heavenly realms rage in battle for the will of God, while those who are under the dragon's command war day and night to thwart the will of God from coming to pass. Caught in the middle of this conflict are you and I. But we have been invited onto the battlefield; we have been charged to clothe ourselves in the "full armor of God" (Eph. 6:11 NASB); we have been commissioned to stand against all the wiles of the enemy; and we have been instructed to extinguish his fiery darts with the shield of faith. The only way you can lose is by believing that you are not in the battle at all. Some people think, *If I leave the devil alone, he will leave me alone!* But there is no guarantee. First Peter 5:8 says, "Be sober, be vigilant; because your adversary the devil walks about like a roaring lion, seeking whom he may devour." Whether you like it or not, the devil is constantly on the prowl looking to destroy, and it's even better for him when someone is unarmed, unaware, and defenseless.

Our battles have already been won in the heavenly realms by Christ Jesus. So why do we need to battle at all then? Because the devil is a thief, and the Christian's job is to *enforce* the victory already won by Christ! This is what PUSH is all about. It's recognizing that the devil has been utterly defeated by the risen Christ, but tragically he continually goes uncontested because people don't know they need to push him back.

Jesus cast out demons. Why? Because they would not leave of their own accord. They had to be cast out. They had no right to oppress and destroy God's people, and yet they do not play by the rules and seek to oppress and destroy them anyway. Jesus had to cast them out using His authority, and so must we—using the authority Christ purchased when He rose from the grave. He is seated above all authority and power and, as a born-again believer, so are you. Pray and enforce the victory of the cross, cast out the devil, bind him, and evict him from your home. The Bible says, "Nor give place to the devil" (Eph. 4:27). Don't let him have one inch!

The Power of the Blood

> For the weapons of our warfare are not carnal but mighty in God for pulling down strongholds, casting down arguments and every high thing that exalts itself against the knowledge of God, bringing every thought into captivity to the obedience of Christ. (2 Cor. 10:4–5)

Let me tell you that you and I have been furnished with very powerful weapons. God has not only delivered us from the power of the devil, but He has also triumphantly set us in power over him! There is one weapon that I believe is like the atomic bomb of Christian warfare. Do you know what it is? It's the blood of the Lamb: "And they overcame him [the devil] by the blood of the Lamb" (Rev. 12:11).

How often do you take communion? Monthly at church, or perhaps weekly? Have you ever taken communion in your home? When God wanted to deliver His people out of Egypt, He had to deal with an obstinate Pharaoh who refused the will of God ten times, and so God had to contend with him ten times, the final time taking his firstborn. The children of Israel were spared any harm because of one thing: the blood of the lamb. The blood of the Lamb is powerful because it satisfies the legal judgment of God upon man's sin, and in doing so completely removes any footing the devil has to oppress, afflict, and torment us. Where there is no sin, there is no judgment. Where there is no sin, the devil has no access. He couldn't wreak havoc on mankind until he moved them to sin against God.

In my early years of ministry, every time I would travel away and minister, something crazy would happen at home. At first I would wear it as a badge, a sort of confirmation that I was certainly troubling the enemy's kingdom and therefore making a difference for God. Heck, if I was really honest, I was kind of honored that I was on his radar— on his hit list! But then one day as I was away ministering, the call came from Leanne, and the distress in her voice told me that something was very wrong. In the past I had simply swept away these problems with a dismissive tone, reminding her that it was just confirmation that we were indeed doing what God had called us to do. The problems were part of the turf, part of the game.

Her voice rose into a higher pitch as she stated that Ashley, my second son, had stopped breathing and had to be rushed to the emergency room. I was so far away, and my beautiful bride had two small children to take care of, and every time I was away a crisis would escalate to just beyond her ability to cope, and this time she was not having it. She demanded I either stop traveling and ministering or I do something to stop things from happening every time I went away.

Annoyed at her lack of faith (I'm embarrassed to say) but gripped with alarm for my son's well-being and recovery, I spoke to the Lord and said, "God, is there anything that can be done? Can you maybe give this woman you gave me a little more faith, or—" Just then God interrupted me and said, *It doesn't have to be like this!* Now He had my attention. *What the blood covers, the enemy* must *pass over!* He immediately drew my attention to the Passover spoken of in the book of Exodus and showed me how the destroyer was sent out to destroy the firstborn children of every home, but he could not penetrate nor come near any home that had the blood of the lamb sprinkled on the doorposts and lintels.

I had always just seen this as a salvation illustration but never applicable for my own household. God showed me that I could completely remove any satanic attack of sickness, disease, pestilence, or destruction the enemy sought to bring upon our house for troubling his. I was amazed. How do I do this? He said, *Apply the blood, take communion in your home with your wife, and apply it to your household!* Leanne was delighted as I shared what God had shown me, that we had power to completely dismiss the devil and his antics. We had power over sickness, oppression, and even our finances.

When the children of Israel came out of Egypt, the Bible says "there was none feeble among His tribes" (Ps. 105:37). About 600,000 people, and not one with so much as a sniffle? Not only that, but they came out with all the silver and gold of Egypt— prosperity. Freedom from oppression, deliverance from bondage, prosperity, and healing were all experienced by the children of Israel because of the blood of the lamb sprinkled on the lintels and doorposts of their homes forcing the destroyer to "pass over"! If that happened by the blood of ordinary lambs and goats, how much more powerful is the blood of the holy Lamb of God, the one John the Baptist pointed out in the gospel of John as "the Lamb of God, who takes away the sin of the world" (1:29)? To this day I have seen supernatural healings, miracles, and incredible blessings and prosperity upon our house because we "apply the blood" at home. We take communion and push the devil out of our domain and jurisdiction.

As a believer it is your right to *enforce* the precious blood of our Savior and push back the destroyer. I cannot even begin to mention the peace, power, and joy this weapon of truth has brought into our lives. Apply the blood of Jesus and see God's supernatural protection manifest in your life!

The Only Prayer God Cannot Answer

Did you know there is a prayer that God just cannot answer? Even with all of His love, graciousness, and benevolence, He simply cannot answer *the prayer that was never prayed*. Therefore, one of the main weapons the enemy brings against us is distraction, getting us too busy to pray. He loves discouragement too, because that one completely removes any motivation to pray. In the Garden of Gethsemane, Jesus told His disciples how troubled and overwhelmed His soul felt by what was about to take place and what He must do for mankind. He asked those guys to spend one hour in prayer for Him. But upon returning from praying to the Father with such intensity and pressure that He was literally sweating drops of blood, He found the disciples sleeping. He woke them and asked them again to spend just an hour in prayer as the "fulfillment of all the ages" was coming down at that moment in time. But after promising they would pray, they were once again overcome by sleep.

Jesus was about to lift the weight of the sins of mankind from our shoulders for all eternity, and the disciples could not lift Him up in prayer for a single hour! Understand the biggest battle I face as a minister of the gospel is not the devil, but my inability to pray when prompted and asked by God. The most powerful people on planet earth are praying people! PUSH people pray when prompted, but sleep will always be the sweet nectar of choice by our flesh.

In case you feel overwhelmed and think, *Man, I'm just like the disciples. I let God down every time He asks me to pray,* let me show you one of the best ways to pray effectively. "For we do not know what we should pray for as we ought, but the Spirit Himself makes intercession for us with groanings which cannot be uttered" (Rom. 8:26). Let the Holy Spirit pray through you!

Prayer Languages

And He said to them, "Go into all the world and preach the gospel to every creature. He who believes and is baptized will be saved; but he who does not believe will be condemned. And these signs will follow those who believe: In My name they will cast out demons; they will speak with new tongues; they will take up serpents; and if they drink anything deadly, it will by no means hurt them; they will lay hands on the sick, and they will recover." (Mark 16:15–18)

What was it that caused the Tower of Babel to cease being built? Was it a lack of resources? Did they run out of money? Was there a famine or plague in the land? Was it poor architectural advice? An earthquake? Was it a strike by the unions? Nope, it was none of these. It was language! When God saw what they were building in opposition to His will (multiply and fill the earth versus let's build a city and make a name for ourselves), He saw that the best way to shut down their project was through language.

He who controls the language has the power. In my state of California, twice it has gone to the ballot to usher in same-sex marriage, and both times it has been voted down. So to sidestep the democratic process a gay activist judge overturned the votes of seven million people. Proponents of same-sex marriage changed the language from "gay marriage" to "same-sex marriage," and still they found overwhelming resistance. In a stroke of shrewd resourcefulness, they changed the language again to "marriage equality." Now media voices are touting that Americans have changed their mores and are much more liberal and open-minded, but the truth is, very little has changed in the hearts of people. They (gay activists) simply changed the language. I mean, who goes around picketing, "I'm all for inequality! I say let's find equality and overthrow it with inequality!" No one wants to be on the side of perceived "inequality." No peace-seeking person wants to tout that they are for prejudice or inequality, and so same-sex marriage found a Trojan horse to get its agenda through the moral gates of Troy!

Make no mistake—language has power. Jesus told the disciples to wait in the upper room in Jerusalem until they received power. When that power manifested itself, it came by way of "speak[ing] with other tongues" (Acts 2:4). What a strange way to distribute power. Yet power it was, because from there Peter preaches and 3,000 people get saved. From there, healings, signs, and wonders accompany the disciples wherever they go. God has power for you. It comes by way of languages you have never learned. All you have to do is receive!

Language: Keeping You Out or Getting You In?

What was it that kept the children of Israel out of the promised land? What was it that got Joshua and Caleb into the promised land? It was language, pure and simple. The children of Israel complained continually, and finally God became so fed up that He told Moses in Numbers 14 that none of the children of Israel would enter into the promised land except Caleb, for he had a different spirit. Complaining is more than just the language of victims; it is the language of injustice, and what you confess you will possess. You cannot enter into God's promises as a victim. Neither can you enter into what God has for you by claiming injustice. We enter the promises of God through faith and patience. That is it!

Language is powerful. In fact, it is a powerful indicator of the condition of your heart. Your language (or words) locate you. Jesus said, "Out of the abundance of the heart the mouth speaks" (Matt. 12:34). In other words, what is in your heart will continually come out of your mouth! That's why God seeks to change our hearts, because the Bible says that we lay hold of this great salvation: "For with the heart one believes unto righteousness, and with the mouth confession is made unto salvation" (Rom. 10:10). Your mouth is a producer, and what you speak about, you bring about. Line your language up with the promises of God and watch what begins to happen.

Languages Unlock

Are there languages that unlock heaven? Are there certain musical notes that unlock the spiritual world?

Before you think this to be a far-fetched question or fanciful notion, let me tell you emphatically that the Bible teaches that not only are there heavenly languages accessible by humans but also that certain music unlocks the heavens, perhaps like the ancient Greek mythological figure of Pan and his magic flute.

The apostle Paul wrote about speaking in the "tongues of men and of angels" in 1 Corinthians 13:1. The Scriptures also teach that when David played music upon his harp, the demonic spirit that was troubling Saul would depart and he would be at peace and become refreshed. The power of God came upon the prophet Elisha to prophesy and bring breakthrough and hope where there was drought, desperation, and fear, because of a musician playing a harp of worship to God:

"But now bring me a musician." Then it happened, when the musician played, that the hand of the LORD came upon him. And he said, "Thus says the Lord: 'Make this valley full of ditches.' For thus says the Lord: 'You shall not see wind, nor shall you see rain; yet that valley shall be filled with water, so that you, your cattle, and your animals may drink.'" (2 Kings 3:15–17)

It has long been believed that Lucifer was created as the angel of worship or music because of the strong language of "pipes and timbrels" created within him on his day of creation: "The workmanship of your timbrels and pipes was prepared for you on the day you were created" (Ezek. 28:13). When we look at the world around us, it is unquestionable that music has the power to shape, influence, and inspire. Even in malls, our favorite fashion retail outlets play music to make the customers feel good and inspired to buy a new item or two or three.

Many experiments have shown the power of classical music and its positive effects on plant life. Dr. Singh, head of botany at Annamalai University in India, conducted some of these studies.

> While listening to classical and baroque music, the plants grew 72 percent more leaves, and they grew 20 percent faster. The plants which were exposed to rock music grew abnormally tall and died in two weeks. The plants which were exposed to classical and baroque music ended up leaning toward the speakers instead of the light, and the closest plants began to wrap themselves around the speakers.[1]

Wouldn't it be like the devil to keep this truth out of the hands of believers while he himself takes on the role of the pied piper and leads generation after generation toward destruction? But PUSH will show you just how powerful these truths are as well as how accessible they are to the believer.

Tiananmen Square, 1989

> Likewise the Spirit also helps in our weaknesses. For we do not know what we should pray for as we ought, but the Spirit Himself makes intercession for us with groanings which cannot be uttered. (Rom. 8:26)

On January 2, 1989, I was invited to a prayer meeting overlooking the city of Wollongong, Australia, where I grew up. That night, amidst a handful of about twenty faithful prayer warriors, I was baptized with the Holy Spirit and began to speak with other tongues. I know that this may be controversial depending upon your denomination and beliefs, but I have to be true to my story, so please forgive me and keep reading.

I was so overcome by the Holy Spirit that night that I could not stop laughing and actually had someone else drive my car home for me (much like a designated driver), because the only way I could describe what I felt was "intoxication." Being new territory for this young Christian, I did not know whether my driving skills would be impaired or not, and since I had a car full of passengers I decided to err on the side of caution.

Upon arriving home, I went straight into my room and began to pray and then opened the Bible. Up until then Bible reading had been quite a chore and more of a duty than a delight. But for the next three hours, I could not put the Bible down. It was like the words were swimming on the page and had come alive with revelation. It was as if something in my understanding opened and instead of the Bible being required reading to pass a test, it became the most gripping novel dispelling truths about the person of God. It was incredible.

Every day I would pray in my new unlearned languages, and it wouldn't be uncommon for an hour or two to slip by without my noticing. But a few months into the year, something strange happened. I was praying in my room and asking God to use me for His purposes on the earth. Just as I did that, I had the tightest knot form in my stomach, and I thought maybe it was something I had eaten that was going to come flying out of my body like a scud missile. But it wasn't indigestion, food poisoning, or appendicitis. Instead, I felt the strongest urge to pray. As I did there was a tangible relieving of the "burden" in my stomach, but when I tried to stop, it returned, so I knew I had to keep praying.

Things became even crazier when all of a sudden I found myself praying in some type of Asian or Chinese dialect. That was weird, and if my unsaved family and atheist dad had stumbled into my room to find me in that state, it would have certainly meant a one-way trip to the psych ward. Yet every time I tried to stop, the burden would return, and I had to pray. After about ninety minutes of that, the burden all of a sudden completely subsided, and I knew I was free. I had prayed through something, and it was the weirdest thing. I asked God to use me, but I wasn't expecting Him to take it quite so literally or dramatically. I wanted to get out of there in case God had some other plans in mind while He had my complete cooperation. So I ran looking for the most unsaved family member in my house, thinking that would keep God at bay.

I ran into the living room, where I saw my dad sitting on the couch watching the evening news. I sat right next to him. Thinking I was safe, I looked at the TV to see what he was watching, and I saw tanks that had been running over people come to a complete halt in front of a wall of student protesters holding hands. Then God spoke to me and said, *You just prayed for that!* Wow, talk about goose bumps. That completely freaked me out!

But it got worse about six months or so later when we had a missionary at our church who told the story about how the protestors stood in front of the tanks willing to give their lives for the cause. The general gave the command to the operators of the tanks to proceed and drive down the protestors, but something strange and supernatural happened. It was like some type of electroshock went through the tanks, because they *all* stalled and could not follow through on the command given them. Just then God spoke to me again and said, *My power is greater than the war machinery of men!* Once again humbled and freaked out all at the same time, I realized we have been given quite an extraordinary gift in prayer. If only we used it more often.

FIVE

The King's Speech

Where the word of a king is, there is power; and
who may say to him, "What are you doing?"
—ECCLESIASTES 8:4

In the 2010 Oscar-winning film *The King's Speech*, actor Colin Firth plays the part of King George VI, whose ascension to the throne of Great Britain would be accompanied by his severe speech impediment. King George knows that to rule effectively and be taken seriously, he must have command over his diction. He hires a speech therapist played by Geoffrey Rush, who gives the king the confidence to enunciate words that he formerly struggled with, helping him to recover both his cadence and his self-assurance. It is an incredibly moving film, one that highlights the importance and power of the spoken word.

God, who is the King of kings, creates everything by the Word of His mouth. In fact, His Word is supreme in the universe. Nothing and no one can undo what He has spoken and what He has declared. In Genesis chapter one, God creates the heavens and the earth, light and life, by nothing more than speaking. His Word is the beginning and the end of all things.

PUSH prayer is prayer that is based upon the Word of God. If you can see God's Word as seed, you will see that within this seed is the will of God. Every seed reproduces after its own kind. It cannot do otherwise. An orange seed cannot produce bananas and an apple seed cannot produce watermelons. This is because within each seed is its DNA. Each word of God contains the DNA of God within it and it is sent forth for no other reason than to establish or bring about His will.

> So shall My word be that goes forth from My mouth; It shall not return to Me void, but it shall accomplish what I please, and it shall prosper in the thing for which I sent it. (Isa. 55:11)

The Word of God is so powerful that the Bible says in Matthew 13 that when the Word of God is sown and the recipient does not understand it, the devil comes immediately and snatches away what was sown (v. 19). The devil is terrified of the Word of God because he has no power over it. However, he has the power to snatch it away and he attacks it, resisting it relentlessly. When we speak God's Word we are engaging in spiritual warfare. The devil hates the Word because it brings forth light and diminishes darkness.

Prayer is most potent when we speak and declare the Word of God. It acts like a battering ram, pushing back the siege walls of the kingdom of darkness. It releases into the atmosphere that which overcomes darkness, bringing forth light. Jesus spoke into a tomb and a dead man walked out. In the middle of a tempest, Jesus stood on the bow of the ship and said "Peace, be still!" and immediately the storm subsided and the sea became as calm and smooth as glass (Mark 4:39). PUSH is prayer that is based upon the Word of God, fueled by the Word of God, carrying the goal of accomplishing the Word of God.

Rhema versus Logos

Faith is the language

> Is anyone among you sick? Let him call for the elders of the church, and let them pray over him, anointing him with oil in the name of the Lord. And the prayer of faith will save the sick, and the Lord will raise him up. And if he has committed sins, he will be forgiven. (James 5:14–15)

Please notice that that verse says "the prayer of faith," not the prayer of sincerity, desperation, hopelessness, religiosity, or piety. It is faith that moves God, not need. It is faith that unlocks the power of heaven in our lives. Faith speaks with declarative tones. Faith is the language of confidence in outcome. Faith is a trust that has been established by getting personally acquainted with the promise and the character of the One who made the promise. Faith calls something done before it is so. Faith speaks those things that are not as though they are (Rom. 4:17).

The prayer of faith is a confident prayer based upon the knowledge of God's promises through His Word. It is prayed from a heart convinced that it is so. It never prays, "If it be Thy will." Not once will you see Jesus or one of the disciples work a miracle or perform a healing by praying, "Lord, if it be Thy will." Yet today's churches are filled with ministers who, having graduated from seminary, pray dead, impotent prayers, not seeing any signs, wonders, or miracles. There is no manifestation of the power of God, and so they adjust and change their theology to line up with their experience.

Faith is Jesus coming to the tomb of Lazarus, his dear friend, only to be confronted by an overwhelmed-with-grief Martha. "Lord, if You had been here, my brother would not have died" was Martha's statement, yet Jesus said to her confidently, "Your brother will rise again" (John 11:21, 23). To that Martha responded—displaying she had some theology, some understanding of the promises of God—"I know that he will rise again in the resurrection at the last day" (v. 24). She's saying, "See, I was listening to your teachings." So Jesus declared, "I am the resurrection" (v. 25). In other words, where I go, resurrection power goes with me. Now let me ask you this: what is your confession of who you are when you face a situation that needs a miracle?

Is this your internal dialogue? *I'm not worthy to ask God to do this! I don't have enough anointing for this kind of miracle. I'm nobody special, just a humble, meek servant who is grateful whether God does a miracle or not.* If this is where you live, then you need to understand that you are undermining or at worst ignorant of what God has done for you in Christ Jesus. The Scripture says that we are "joint heirs with Christ" (Rom. 8:17). The Bible says in Ephesians that we are seated with Christ in the heavenly places far above every principality and power (1:20–21) and we are to pray from our seated place of authority and power (Eph. 2:5–6). Anything less is a travesty of biblical knowledge. Hosea was right when he prophesied, "My people are destroyed for lack of knowledge" (4:6). Let me say it again: what you don't know can hurt you! In fact, what you don't know *is* hurting you.

God did not say to Moses, "Pray and beg me to release the children of Israel from their bondage to Pharoah." No, God said to Moses, "Go and say to Pharoah, *let my people go*!" Authority is confidence. The first thing God had to heal or repair or perhaps even establish in Moses was *who* he was. Moses said, "Who am I that I should go to Pharoah?" (Ex. 3:11). Before he could speak with authority and power to deliver God's will into the earth, Moses had to come to a realization of who he was in God. Do you know who you are in God?

A *voice of triumph!*

We are caught in time. There is a time coming when time will be no more. Until then we are living in a world governed by time. God has set these times and seasons by His own authority, mainly to put an end to sin and death. He threw the devil to earth from heaven and then thrust him into time so that evil would have an expiration date. The time we are living in is outlined in Psalm 110:1: "The LORD said to my Lord, 'Sit at My right hand, till I make Your enemies Your footstool.'"

We are living in the age when God's enemies are very real and present but are being subdued under Christ's feet. How does this happen? The psalmist says in the very next verse, "The LORD shall send the rod of Your strength out of Zion. Rule in the midst of Your enemies!" (Ps. 110:2). The "rod" in Scripture is a symbol of authority. The Red Sea parted when Moses stretched out his rod.

When Moses walked into Pharaoh's court, Pharaoh was the highest authority in the land, in fact in the world at that time. But Moses was given a rod from God that carried a higher authority than that of Pharaoh, and God said, *Let the showdown begin!* He was showing Moses that though Israel had been under bondage and slavery to this authority and power, there was a higher authority and greater power at work in the earth that desired to deliver the Israelites to freedom.

You may be sitting there reading this thinking to yourself, *Man, I wish God would give me a rod of authority!* I have some great news for you. That's exactly what God has done for you and me. The rod for you and me as we live in the New Testament era is the name of Jesus. God has put everything under His feet and has given Him the name that is above every name, that at that name every knee shall bend, every tongue shall confess that Jesus Christ is Lord, in heaven, on earth, and under the earth. That's powerful! We are called to use the name of Jesus like Moses used the rod, to bring Christ's enemies into subjection to His authority and to deliver God's people to freedom.

When you pray begging prayers, there is no push, but when you pray with an awareness of the authority in the name of Jesus, you will begin to see things shift and devils bow. It is not about being confident for confidence's sake. It is about being confident in who Christ is and who you are in Him. Victory in this life is experienced positionally, not circumstantially! We pray from a heavenly place, seated in Christ, and we are given the rod of the highest authority—the name of Jesus. Jesus said, "These signs will follow those who believe: In My name they will cast out demons" (Mark 16:17).

The Scripture adjures us to cry out to God with a *voice of triumph*. Interestingly, it does not say a voice of passivity, dependency, or feebleness. You will pray with a voice of triumph when you know who God is, what He has promised you, and what His will is in your situation. I am not talking about praying in presumption. I am talking about getting to know God through the medium of His revealed Word, the Bible, and becoming familiar with God's ways. The Bible says the children of Israel knew His acts, but Moses knew His ways. *Acts* are after the event; *ways* are before the event. Most Christians who are ignorant of God's Word and promises lose their prophetic edge and live in the past, only ever experiencing God's acts, usually in the form of hearing about God's mighty acts in other people's lives while they become bewildered, wondering why God is so absent in their lives.

Moses knew God and therefore knew His ways, which meant he lived prophetically and confidently because He knew the ways of God. He was able to intercede. At the Red Sea he was able to speak and prophesy when there was no natural or visible sign of hope: "Stand still, and see the salvation of the LORD, which He will accomplish for you today. For the Egyptians whom you see today, you shall see again no more forever" (Ex. 14:13). How did Moses know that? Was it presumption, or perhaps a lucky guess? No, it was as good as done because Moses knew God and therefore knew God's ways! "The people who know their God shall be strong, and carry out great exploits" (Dan. 11:32).

Elijah found his prayer voice at Mount Carmel and defeated 450 prophets of Baal, bringing an entire nation to its knees. John the Baptist found that he was a voice in the wilderness crying,

"Make straight the paths of God," and when God sent His Word into the world it rested upon John (Luke 3:4). Moses found his prayer voice enabling him to command the most powerful man on the earth to let God's people go! Have you found your prayer voice? Impossibility begins to diminish for the man or woman who has found this voice. However, you cannot buy this voice on a Christian TV channel, nor can you copy someone who already has one. This voice is found and produced in the wilderness. John was in the wilderness until the day of his manifestation to Israel. Elijah was in the wilderness until his emergence. Moses was in the wilderness when at the burning bush he discovered and developed his prayer voice.

Become a voice to your generation. Seek Him in your wilderness. Pay the price and end up with something the earth cannot annul and demons cannot overthrow.

SIX

The Silence of the Lambs

Why do you cry to Me? Tell the children of
Israel to go forward. But lift up your rod, and
stretch out your hand over the sea and divide
it. And the children of Israel shall go on dry
ground through the midst of the sea.
—EXODUS 14:15–16

It almost sounds like a contradiction if you're writing a book entitled *PUSH: Pray Until Something Happens*, to then turn around and write an entire chapter on when not to pray. But if you will hear me out, I believe you will experience some incredible insight that will help you push and breakthrough into God's perfect will for your life. Sometimes it's an act of obedience, faith, a declaration, or just one word spoken with authority that will push back the opposing powers of darkness and release the promises of God over your life.

When I say there are times not to pray, I mean it in the context of what has come to be known as traditional prayer—namely *hopelessly begging* God's interest and intervention without any real guarantee. God has not set us up to be so overwhelmed by life and its opposing forces, challenges, and setbacks that He somehow revels in having people beg for His intervention. If this is how you have come to see God, you are reading the right book. *It is your Father's good pleasure to give you the kingdom* (Luke 12:32, emphasis added). But more than that, it was God's original intention in Genesis to give you might and dominion over all that His hands fashioned.

> For assuredly, I say to you, whoever says to this mountain, "Be removed and be cast into the sea," and does not doubt in his heart, but believes that those things he says will be done, he will have whatever he says. Therefore I say to you, whatever things you ask when you pray, believe that you receive them, and you will have them. (Mark 11:23–24)

Three times in the above verse "says" is mentioned, but only once is "pray" mentioned. We need to understand that the world we live in is shaped and governed by the words that come out of our mouths. You cannot pray in faith and then confess defeat with your mouth. God spoke to Joshua about succeeding Moses and the crux of this instruction was what he meditated upon, and what he spoke out of that meditation would determine his success and prosperity. I believe too many people don't achieve all that they could because they don't push themselves into speaking according to the Word of God as opposed to speaking according to their feelings.

Why Are You Praying?

Moses had just led about 600,000 Israelites to the Red Sea. Out of bondage, out of ten generations of slavery to Pharaoh and his harsh taskmasters. Pharaoh, having realized he had just allowed his entire labor force to depart, decided to send out his military to capture and return them to their barracks and to their duties—namely building his empire and legacy! The most powerful nation on the earth at that time was Egypt. They were the wealthiest and the mightiest nation in the land, with a military far superior to all the other nations of the world.

The children of Israel had reached an impasse to their grand plans of escaping from Pharaoh and entering into a land of their own—a land where they could eat and enjoy the rewards of their own labor and not be laboring for the profit of others while they simply subsisted. It was an incredible impediment to what had been a remarkably smooth journey. All of a sudden the ground beneath their feet began to rumble, and a dust cloud resembling an incoming tempest began to melt away whatever courage they had. Egypt's chariots pursued them.

The children of Israel cried out to Moses, and I want you to notice the difference between Moses' words and the words of the children of Israel:

> And when Pharaoh drew near, the children of Israel lifted their eyes, and behold, the Egyptians marched after them. So they were very afraid, and the children of Israel cried out to the

Lord. Then they said to Moses, "Because there were no graves in Egypt, have you taken us away to die in the wilderness? Why have you so dealt with us, to bring us up out of Egypt? Is this not the word that we told you in Egypt, saying, 'Let us alone that we may serve the Egyptians'? For it would have been better for us to serve the Egyptians than that we should die in the wilderness."

And Moses said to the people, "Do not be afraid. Stand still, and see the salvation of the Lord, which He will accomplish for you today. For the Egyptians whom you see today, you shall see again no more forever. The Lord will fight for you, and you shall hold your peace."

And the Lord said to Moses, "Why do you cry to Me? Tell the children of Israel to go forward. But lift up your rod, and stretch out your hand over the sea and divide it. And the children of Israel shall go on dry ground through the midst of the sea." (Ex. 14:10–16)

But the most important words in that passage of Scripture are what the Lord said to Moses. God said, "Quit praying and start stretching!" The Bible declares "faith without works is dead" (James 2:20). There is a time not to pray. It is the time to exercise the authority that God has given you.

1. "Lift up your rod." In other words, submit to God as in, "Submit to God. Resist the devil and he will flee from you" (James 4:7). Lifting the rod is an act of worship; crudely translated it means "acknowledge God as your source and strength." Once you are connected to God and submitted to God, His authority can and will flow

through you. Remember the Bible behooves us to "be strong in the Lord and in the power of His might" (Eph. 6:10). Nowhere does the Bible teach us to be strong in our own might and strength.

2. "Stretch out your hand over the sea and divide it." I love that. Submit, acknowledge, and worship the God of the impossible, and then stretch out your hand and do the impossible! It was not God's hand that parted the sea; it was Moses' hand. That's going to be a problem for a lot of religious folks. We don't want to believe it because we don't want to carry that kind of responsibility. We'd rather ask God to do it, and when it doesn't happen, we say, "Well, it mustn't have been His will. He's probably taking us back to Egypt to humble us so He can teach us something."

God clearly shows Moses that because he has the rod in his hand, lifted unto the Lord, he can stretch out his hand over the waters and part the sea. God did the miracle through Moses' hands. Never underestimate the power of a submitted life. Some folks reading this might scoff and say, "It wouldn't work for me, lifting a stick, then parting the water in my swimming pool. Yeah, right!" But hear me out. Moses is not a Vegas entertainer, nor is he doing party tricks to amuse himself. He has the *responsibility* of carrying out God's promise to deliver the Israelites out of slavery, into a land flowing with milk and honey. In the kingdom your authority and your responsibility go hand in hand. But the other factor that draws God's power into our lives is our devotion to seeing His will and not our own will come to pass.

Moses had a word from God, had the rod in his hand, and was in a place not of his choosing but of his obedience. So when God said, "Stretch out your hand and part the sea," that man had undiluted power flowing from the throne right through his hand and out over the sea. Obedience is power. Submission is strength.

Jesus at Lazarus's Tomb

When Jesus came to the tomb where his dear friend Lazarus had been buried four days earlier, the Bible says Jesus did the same thing as we saw Moses do. Jesus looked up to heaven and prayed (connected with God the Father, His source). Then He spoke in a loud voice, "Lazarus, come forth!" and the dead man came back to life (John 11:43–44). Jesus did not pray, "Lord, we just ask that if it be Thy will that Thou wouldst raise up Lazarus from the dead, but if not, Lord, help us to learn something from this loss today and accept it as Thy will." I promise you if Jesus would have prayed that prayer, nothing would have happened that day. Jesus knew the will of God, knew who He was in God, and then He spoke with authority over the grave and Lazarus's decomposing corpse and brought life where there was death, decay, and corruption.

Prayer Aligns Us

When we face challenges that overwhelm us, we become dis-combobulated and begin to question ourselves, God, and our circumstances. Prayer is then the essential tool to bring us back into alignment with who we are in God, what His Word promises us, and where He has positioned us by His own doing, not our performance. Prayer is vital to reestablish and remind us who we are in Him, what He has promised, and how powerful His Word is in our mouths. We just need to speak to our mountain: "For assuredly, I say to you, whoever says to this mountain, 'Be removed and be cast into the sea,' and does not doubt in his heart, but believes that those things he says will be done, he will have whatever he says" (Mark 11:23).

Jesus did not say that if we pray the mountain would move. He did not say, "Pray to the Father to move the mountain." He said you and I are to speak in faith and if we believe that what we said has power, it will happen. The only way we can believe we have power is by knowing who we are in Christ, where we are seated, and what God has given us dominion over.

You Do Something About It

There is one miracle that is recorded in all four gospels. It's the feeding of the five thousand. Once again the miracle begins with a massive problem. The disciples feel that Jesus has gotten a little carried away with His teaching and preaching and kept the people a couple of days, and they have eaten everything they brought with them. The disciples try to gently rebuke Jesus and ask Him to let the people go so they can buy food for themselves before all the markets and stores close in the surrounding neighborhood. Jesus turns to the disciples and says to them, "You give them something to eat!"

Taken aback at the audacity of Jesus asking them to do the impossible, they begin to make excuses. However, Jesus didn't just teach; He also believed that with God nothing was impossible. So he kept looking, until finally Andrew piped up and said, "There is a lad here who has five barley loaves and two small fish, but what are they among so many?" (John 6:9). Jesus knew exactly what they were among so many—an opportunity for God to move. So He instructed them to seat the crowds into groups of fifty. The disciples looked at each other and wondered whether Jesus had heat stroke, or whether someone had put something in His water, but the very serious expression on His face told them they'd better do it anyway.

Jesus took the five loaves and two fish and, looking up to heaven, gave thanks. Note that, like with Moses, the first part of pushing into a miracle is looking to heaven. Connecting with heaven. Not looking at the impossibility of the problem or situation.

Then He blessed it and broke it. Whatever is blessed multiplies.

Then He stretched out his hands and handed the food to the disciples and instructed them to stretch out their hands and give to the multitudes, and the bread and fish miraculously multiplied. Submit to God and stretch out your hand. Push!

We push from our God connection or God place. Sometimes it's a word that we are prompted to speak out in a prophetic proclamation that will shift things in our world. When one of my kids was under incredible attack from the evil one who was trying to destroy his life, Leanne and I prayed like you would not believe. As we were praying, a word (Scripture) came to me from the Lord, and we began to speak out loud in a bold declaration what God had put into our hearts. What had been a struggle for years became a breakthrough in a matter of days—because the Word of God is the most powerful force in the universe, bringing light despite the presence of darkness.

Psalm 119:89 says, "Forever, O LORD, Your word is settled in heaven." The word *settled* is a Hebrew word and is used when an army takes a plot of land or territory and then appoints sentinels to guard that territory. When we speak the Word of God into our situation, it seizes and recovers lost territory, and there's nothing the devil can do to stop it—just like the darkness could not stop the light from manifesting. The only way darkness can prevail is to prevent the Word from being spoken.

Authority Over Nations and Kingdoms

Whether you realize this or not, you have been given access to an authority over the nations and the kingdoms of this world. Look at these scriptures:

Then God said, "Let there be light"; and there was light. (Gen. 1:3)

Then the LORD put forth His hand and touched my mouth, and the LORD said to me: "Behold, I have put My words in your mouth. See, I have this day set you over the nations and over the kingdoms, to root out and to pull down, to destroy and to throw down, to build and to plant." (Jer. 1:9–10)

What is it that can set Jeremiah, you, and me over the nations and over the kingdoms? It's the Word of God in our mouths!

Sun, Stand Still

Joshua had the massive task of being Moses' successor. To make it even more stupendous, God did not give him a magic stick like He did for Moses. Instead, God instructed him to "be strong and very courageous . . . This Book of the Law shall not depart from your mouth, but you shall meditate in it day and night, that you may observe to do according to all that is written in it. For then you will make your way prosperous, and then you will have good success" (Josh. 1:7, 8). Joshua wasn't given a magic stick. He was given something even more powerful. He was told to meditate in the Word of God and to not let it depart from his mouth. In other words, *speak the Word*.

It is the Word of God that has power over the nations and kingdoms. God's Word is not subject to nations or kingdoms because His Word is *above* everything. It is greater than the darkness. It is greater than any storm or wind. It is greater than the devil. It is the most powerful creative force in the universe. When it is in our mouth, it is as powerful as it is in God's mouth, because it is the Word of God. That's what a prophet is, a person who has God's Word in his or her mouth. God's Word is backed up by God's power. In fact, God's Word releases God's power. Joshua came to Gibeon's aid against eight kings who had formed an alliance to resist the children of Israel's advances, and as the battle raged, the hour began to get late so that it looked like time would be against them and keep them from utterly defeating the enemy.

> Then Joshua spoke to the Lord in the day when the Lord delivered up the Amorites before the children of Israel, and he said in the sight of Israel: "Sun, stand still over Gibeon; and Moon, in the Valley of Aijalon." So the sun stood still, and the moon stopped, till the people had revenge upon their enemies. Is this not written in the Book of Jasher? So the sun stood still in the midst of heaven, and did not hasten to go down for about a whole day. (Josh. 10:12–13)

Joshua did not have a magic stick because he did not need one. He had the Word of God in his mouth. When God's Word is in your mouth, there is nothing that any power can do to thwart it.

SEVEN

The LORD of the Rings

*Prayer is not getting man's will done in heaven, but
getting God's will done on earth. It is not overcoming
God's reluctance but laying hold of God's willingness.*
—RICHARD C. TRENCH

Next to *Star Wars*, my favorite trilogy is the *Lord of the Rings*.
Hobbits, Elves, Dwarves, Orcs, the all-seeing eye of Sauron trying to locate the one ring that rules all rings, and a grotesque
creature named for his horrible throaty cough—Gollum—all set
the stage for a very entertaining time. J. R. R Tolkien was a genius
for sure. Battles rage and adventure drips through every moment
of the journey; insurmountable odds are faced; trials and disap-
pointments are overcome; betrayal and deception experienced, all
to carry about a great mission.

We, too, are called to such a great adventure. In fact, it is my
belief that Tolkien, a practicing Christian, was bringing spiritual
kingdom realities to life through the medium of stories for the
emerging generation(s). There are sinister forces of evil trying to
plunge the world we know into chaos and darkness. It seeks to

ensnare and enslave mankind, making them Satan's subjects, sub-jugated by their own appetites and desires. This is our battle. We stand in the breach: we are it; we stand as the last line of defense between peace and destruction. It has been this way since a carpen-ter's son from Nazareth declared upon the mount, "You are the salt of the earth . . . you are the light of the world" (Matt. 5:13, 14). If we PUSH in prayer, God results happen. If we are silent, then the enemy triumphs. It's that simple.

We have established that there are two kingdoms in conflict here on earth and that we are indeed engaged in a battle. One seeks to bring about our heavenly Father's will, while evil forces seek to oppose His will and reign here on the earth. That is predominantly why PUSH is required. It is *not* that God is reluctant in answering prayer; it is that the enemy is resistant!

The Bible has a very simple formula for PUSH that I want to show you.

> Far be it from You to do such a thing as this, to slay the righ-teous with the wicked, so that the righteous should be as the wicked; far be it from You! Shall not the Judge of all the earth do right? (Gen. 18:25)

Now let's talk about changing God's mind.

What? You read that correctly. I love writing that headline, and even more than writing it I like to preach it. It always draws a potent reaction from those who have neatly laid God in their theological casket. It's amazing how many folks feel threatened about the possibility of God changing His mind, because they see it as a crack in His sovereignty, and therefore in their security that "everything that happens is meant to be."

God is secure in His sovereignty, for he "is not a man, that He should lie, nor a son of man, that He should repent" (Num. 23:19). But we know that God often changes His mind and even relents. *Repent* and *relent* are two completely different words and have two completely different meanings. (Relent: *abandon or mitigate a harsh intention or cruel treatment.* Repent: *feel or express sincere regret or remorse about one's wrongdoing or sin.*) God does not repent because He does not sin and is incapable of wrongdoing. This is one of the things that makes Him so magnificent. He does, however, "relent" again and again throughout the Scripture of judgment or a harsh intention in His wrath.

In Genesis 18, Abraham interceded for Sodom and Gomorrah, which God had determined He would destroy in righteous judgment for their wickedness. God was not throwing a tantrum or overreacting to a few minor scandals. This is righteous judgment on a city that had become so perverse that when two angels visited the city, men surrounded the house they entered and demanded to have sex with them. The owner of the house, who was the most righteous man in the city, offered the band of perverted men his virgin daughters in an attempt to persuade them away from their perversion, to which the men reacted with violent threats, saying, "We will deal worse with you than with them" (Gen. 19:9). Nice people. Sounds like a great place to visit.

Yet Abraham interceded for the city, specifically for his nephew Lot whom he knew was living within its walls. God relented from His "plan A" to wipe out the entire city with all its infected inhabitants to a "plan B," where Lot and his family became the beneficiaries of God's grace and were saved in the midst of the destruction. Had Abraham *not* interceded, Lot would have perished. His intercessory prayer released God's grace upon Lot and his family. The same still happens today.

The devil will convince you that your son or daughter who is on drugs deserves death, calamity, or some other judgment of God, but the devil is a shrewd prosecution attorney who does not disclose the complete truth—he only speaks in partial truths. While that may be right, the heart of God desires mercy, not judgment; and when you intercede for your son or daughter, you move him or her from God's judgment to God's mercy.

Psalm 89:14 says, "Righteousness and justice are the foundation of Your throne; mercy and truth go before Your face." There are two sides of God's throne—one side is judgment, the other mercy. Intercession has the power to move people from one side to the other. The Bible says that mercy and truth go before His face. We decide whether we are greeted with mercy or with truth. If you embrace Christ as your Lord and Savior, then you have embraced truth, and therefore grace is extended to you from the throne. But those who reject Christ reject truth, and therefore miss out on grace and will have to endure truth when they stand before the throne of God.

When Jonah preached judgment in Nineveh, the king

proclaimed a fast throughout the land and the entire nation repented. What happened next? God relented of His intended judgment and spared the Ninevites, but Jonah the judgment preacher got angry!

I love the story of King Hezekiah. The prophet Isaiah was sent to his house and told the king to set his house in order, as he was going to die of the sickness with which he was afflicted. Upon receiving the word of the Lord, the king cried out to God and repented. Then the Lord spoke to Isaiah and told him to go back to the king—God had changed His mind and would extend his life by fifteen years.

The Bible is full of God seemingly changing His mind. What is actually taking place is God willingly moving people from judgment to mercy because there are folks who know His heart and choose to intercede. The whole point of Jesus coming to die upon the cross should be proof enough that God does not desire to give us what we deserve. Listen to Jesus' harsh rebuke of the "judgment junkies" of His day: "But go and learn what this means: 'I desire mercy, not sacrifice.' For I have not come to call the righteous, but sinners" (Matt. 9:13 NIV).

Prayer shifts people from God's judgment to God's mercy. It's so powerful, and it is so essential. If you don't have a prayer meeting in your church, ask your pastor if you can start one. Don't become that church that has given up hope in the grace and mercy of God and stands there condemning your city because of its sinfulness. Instead, begin to cry out for your city and intercede, moving people from the judgment of God to the mercy of God!

They Don't Deserve Mercy

Many years ago I heard the story of a young man who fled in the heat of the battle in one of Napoleon Bonaparte's conquests. The punishment for cowardice was death. The young man was to be hanged. He was eighteen years old and the only son of a widow. The mother came out on the day he was to be hanged, and there Napoleon stood before the gallows to not only witness the judgment but to approve of it and send a message to one and all that cowardice in battle would not be tolerated. As the young man was led up the rickety wooden stairs, his eyes frantically searched the crowd for his mother, desiring one last look of love before his demise, as the chants and sneers of the crowd bellowed in his ears. Suddenly a woman burst through the barricade and lunged at Napoleon, fastening herself to his feet and crying out, "Have mercy on my son! I beg of you, please have mercy!"

One of Napoleon's guards beat her with the end of his musket, but she fastened herself to the emperor all the more and once again cried out, "Please have mercy upon my son. I beg of you, have mercy!" Napoleon stayed the hand of his guard and spoke with indignation and authority, "Your son does not deserve mercy!" At that the mother replied, "I know. If he deserved it, it would not be mercy!" Upon hearing those words, Napoleon was so rocked that he not only realized mercy is undeserved but he spared the life of the young man and returned him to his mother.

When you and I pray, when we intercede, we pray to a God who *does* understand mercy, not just judgment. Will you pray? Please don't give up on your loved ones, your friends, your city, your community. If we pray, we can see salvation! There are conflicting doctrines in the church today, so let's look at what Jesus taught, as He should trump any other historical figure.

Twenty-First-Century Theological Conflict

Recently I saw a photograph of an incredibly malnourished African child's hand laying limp and almost lifeless in the hand of what appeared to be a white, healthy adult male. The caption below read something along the lines of "Thank God for Missionaries!" Without thinking too much about it, I decided to retweet it, championing missionaries all over the world who selflessly go into undesirable locations with no other agenda but to bring relief. To my surprise, just moments later I received a scathing tweet reply saying, "Missionary? Why doesn't God do something about it, He's all powerful isn't he?" *Okay*, I thought, *fair comment*, and proceeded to reply that poverty and famine in many of these nations are not the result of God's inactivity but rather man's corruption and greed. Many of these nations have suffered at the hands of one dictatorship after another, plundering the nation's wealth and resources. Within moments I was in a Twitter duel. The reply came saying, "Either God is good or He is all powerful. He cannot be both. There are so many people suffering in our world and He does nothing!"

This is largely the fallout of the belief that because God is sovereign it means that He is controlling each and every circumstance down to the minutest detail. It comes from the belief that because God is all-powerful nothing happens outside of His will. Sadly this is rooted in very poor but still very popular theology. I responded by saying that even though the police force have the full authority to enforce the law it does not stop people from committing crimes, and the fact that there are crimes happening does not negate the authority of the law that the police uphold.

If God's will were automatically done why would Jesus instruct His followers to pray that God's will be done on earth as it is in heaven? A kingdom is unlike a democracy. In a democracy the people, through the medium of the popular vote, declare the laws and conditions they wish to be ruled by. Be that good or bad. That's democracy. However, in a kingdom there is only one vote: the king's, because it is his kingdom. Therefore in a kingdom it is the king's will that is done. That's why Jesus in the Lord's Prayer links "Thy kingdom come" with "Thy will be done." The two are interconnected. Where His will is done, His kingdom is come. Where His will is resisted, His kingdom is yet to come. Satan also has a kingdom, and God's will is not on his agenda.

How do you know if you're in the kingdom of God? It's really simple: whose will governs your life? Whose will are you doing— yours or God's? Jesus instructs us that when we pray we are to (1) recognize the existence of the kingdom of God, (2) see its desire to come and be established on the earth, and (3) see that it is being resisted. It becomes established in the hearts of men and women when they turn to Him in their hearts and say, "Not my will, but Thy will be done in my life!" Some call this revival. Whatever you call it, this is what we ought to be praying for. This is the purpose of prayer.

When people ask why bad things happen like murder, rape,

war, and other atrocities, the answer is a very simple one: because God's will is not done here on earth—sadly other wills are at play and are having expression. I think of the song "Amazing Grace," written by a man who once was a slave trader, who kidnapped men, women, and children from their families, put them on ships, and sold them into all kinds of hellish servitude so that he could profit. However, one night while at sea returning from the Ivory Coast of Africa with a ship full of slaves, he encountered the mother of all storms. Fearing for his life, he fell to his knees and begged God to spare his life and his ship from being broken up and he would certainly give up this evil practice. Upon miraculously surviving the storm, John Newton surrendered his life to Jesus Christ and gave up the slave trade, and then proceeded to pen the amazing words, "Amazing grace, how sweet the sound, that saved a wretch like me. I once was lost but now am found, was blind, but now I see."

God has given us a choice to walk in His commandments and statutes or to walk in our own. When we walk in His commands we walk in life, love, and blessing. When we reject them and walk in the dark desires of our souls, pain, misery, and regret are not far behind. Because we as humans are born with Adam's sinful nature we choose self pleasing over God pleasing! So God continually looks for an intercessor to bring His will to pass on the earth. This is the objective of prayer: to be a servant and vehicle of God to bring His will to pass right here, right now. Without prayer nothing happens. With prayer *anything* can happen:

> The people of the land have used oppressions, committed robbery, and mistreated the poor and needy; and they wrongfully

oppress the stranger. So I sought for a man among them who would make a wall, and stand in the gap before Me on behalf of the land, that I should not destroy it; but I found no one. Therefore I have poured out My indignation on them; I have consumed them with the fire of My wrath; and I have recompensed their deeds on their own heads," says the LORD GOD. (Ezek. 22:29–31)

Wow! Did you see the heart of God and the dilemma of God? Because He is holy and just, He cannot turn a blind eye to evil and wickedness but must punish accordingly. The city was full of corruption and wickedness, thus making it a target of God's wrath and judgment. But God instead looked for an intercessor (like Moses interceding for Sodom and Gomorrah) so that He might not destroy the city. All He was looking for was one person, just one, who would build a wall and stand in the gap on behalf of the city, but sadly He found no one and ended up having to pour out His indignation upon the city!

The following story illustrates today's most popular belief when it comes to the will of God:

There was a merchant in Baghdad who sent his servant to market to buy provisions and in a little while the servant came back, white and trembling, and said, "Master, just now when I was in the marketplace I was jostled by a woman in the crowd and when I turned I saw it was Death that jostled me. She looked at me and made a threatening gesture. Now, lend me your horse, and I will ride away from this city and avoid my

fate. I will go to Samarra and there Death will not find me."
The merchant lent him his horse, and the servant mounted it,
and he dug his spurs in its flanks and as fast as the horse could
gallop he went.

Then the merchant went down to the marketplace, and
there he saw Death standing in the crowd. He approached
Death and said, "Why did you make a threatening gesture to
my servant when you saw him this morning?"

"That was not a threatening gesture," replied Death, "it
was only that of complete surprise. I was astonished to see him
in Baghdad, for I have an appointment with him tonight in
Samarra."[1]

This story is actually an adaptation of one of the Solomonic
fables in Jewish antiquity, the point being that not even Solomon
(the wisest man who ever lived) would be able to cheat death/fate.
But is God's will set in stone? Is it removed from the influence and
pleas of men? PUSH is going to radically challenge these positions,
provoking you through the Scriptures to rethink your position on
these things and launch you into powerhouse praying.

If Ignorance Is Bliss, Then Bliss Is Harmful!

Having not grown up in a churchgoing family, I still bear the blessing of understanding community outside of our relatives, because
we were immigrants to Australia from Germany. We would join
with hundreds of other families each Sunday at the German club.

Everyone bore strikingly similar stories of hardship and risking it all to trek to the other side of the world in the hope that they could better support their families. My Sundays were filled with fighting with my mother over her desire to have me wear lederhosen (leather shorts) with braces (suspenders), socks pulled up to my knees, and sandals.

After suffering through a beating or two, I would be able to get out the door wearing shorts with my socks pulled up to my knees and sandals. At the German club the parents would smoke, drink beer, and be entertained by an oompa-loompa band and a German dance team who reveled in slapping each other. So we would band with the other kids and commiserate on our German origin woes together!

One of my friends had a father who worked for a household appliance store, and he was the store manager. This meant that he would often bring the old fridge boxes home for us to play with in the backyard. To say it was awesome would be an understatement. We would gather rocks and make bows and arrows, slingshots, and other projectile devices that could easily remove an eye, and we would shoot and then retreat into the safety of the impenetrable fortress otherwise known as a fridge box! We would play for hours or until someone bled from a direct headshot, but all I can remember is the feeling of invincibility I felt within the box, even when all the other players decided to gang up on me. We could hear the thud of the rocks and projectiles hitting the cardboard, but inside we were completely safe. All we had to do was weather the storm until they ran out of ammo, and then we could surface and pelt our stones at them. It was so much fun. Probably dangerous fun, but this was the eighties and we had never heard the saying, "It's all fun until someone loses an eye!"

One day, my German friend's neighbor asked if he could take the box home with him. Of course it being just a cardboard box and being quite damaged, my friend readily obliged. Sadly, he did not know what would happen next. The kid was a couple of years younger than us and did something so foolish. He decided to get into the box in the middle of the street in front of his house. I can only imagine him experiencing the euphoric feelings that here inside this box was his fortress. In here he was completely safe from all harm. What he couldn't see couldn't hurt him.

A large truck and trailer came hurtling down the street, the truck driver completely unaware that this box had a young boy inside it. The truck went right over the top of the box, severely injuring the young kid and leaving him a quadriplegic with severe brain damage.

My friend's ignorance was certainly not bliss! There are so many people today who live in a cardboard box of theological ignorance, not realizing that a truck called truth and reality is approaching. What you don't know *can* and *will* hurt you!

You Can Be Sincere but Also Be Sincerely Wrong

One of my very early conversion memories is an argument I had with a person over his belief about God and the universe. He was very sincere in his belief that God was in the rocks and that all rocks carry a "god energy," and if we were to wear more crystals and learn to be kind to Mother Nature, then we would in turn attract good energy or good vibes, thus creating harmony in the universe. He was so sincere in his belief, but when I asked him for a historical or theological foundation for his belief system, he came up short. He believed sincerely, yet he was sincerely mistaken. God is a personal being who has revealed Himself through both creation and His Word. He clothed Himself in flesh and stepped into human history, splitting time in half—BC and AD. Sadly there are many people who call themselves Christians, or folks who have grown up in a Christian nation, who are just as sincere in their beliefs—but are also sincerely wrong.

Let me show you a few that I have come across. In the presidential election of 2012, the Republican Party faced some incredible heat over two statements that were made by two of their political leaders regarding rape. Richard Mourdock said, "Life is a gift from God, and if it comes about as a result of rape then it is something God intended to happen."[2] At almost the same time another congressman, Todd Akin, made a similar statement. Other statements you may have heard before containing sincere and strong beliefs around issues of life and mortality go something like this:

- "He must have achieved all he was meant to achieve in this life, so God took him home!" (The friend of a young father of two who drowned in a freak accident)
- "When your number's up, your number's up!" (A twenty-two-year-old college grad whose friend was killed driving home from the graduation ceremony)
- "If it's meant to be, it's meant to be!" (Said of a diving

expedition that went wrong. A twenty-seven-year-old married man drowned.)

- "You can't stand in the way of fate! If your time's up, your time's up!" (Friend of an eighteen-year-old pedestrian killed by a drunk driver)
- "I got this cancer because God obviously wanted to teach me something."

No doubt you have heard some of these sayings when speaking with someone about the death of a loved one. As human beings we want to rationalize, or better yet generalize, why bad things happen. But is there really an expiration date fixed by the universe for our lives? Is our death programmed into the giant cogs of chronological time before we are even born? Are we all living with an invisible egg timer running out the sand? Does God really appoint a day of death for us that we have no fight or say over? Is it already preordained? From the comments above taken directly from conversations I have had with people grappling to make sense of a tragedy or the death of a loved one, you would certainly think so. But is God's will set in stone? To many people it has been taught as being both unknowable and unchangeable.

The Difference Between Taken and Received

Perhaps one of the saddest tragedies I have ever had to deal with in my youth pastor days was the devastation of a young person committing suicide. I am not sure if there is anything more difficult for a family to deal with than the perpetual unanswered question of why? The unceasing reflections of possibilities that could have prevented such a thing from happening, the possible interventions that could have taken place, and the overwhelming feeling of finality and loss of never being able to hold that person again. Some believe it's the ultimate unforgivable sin, sending you to hell because upon taking your life you lose the ability to repent and therefore lose any hope of being forgiven.

I received a call that one of our amazing young youth leaders had succumbed to the unremitting internal struggles she had been facing and had taken her life. Numb with shock, I could only think of the family and the devastation and pain they must be feeling. The young lady was one of the most gifted, beautiful, and intelligent people I had ever met. It just didn't make sense. I was asked to say a few words at the funeral and became overwhelmed at the thought of providing something comforting to a family overcome by grief and despair. I spent the entire day in prayer, crying out to God, my own theological conflict haunting me with more questions than answers. What would I say? What really does happen in a situation like this? Is it really the unforgivable sin? The Bible says that only the blasphemy of the Holy Spirit is unforgivable, but how does one repent after taking one's own life? I desperately cried out to God for both answers and personal consolation. Nothing came.

The night before the funeral, I had a dream where I saw the young lady come running up to me with her usual animated personality, that childlike happy face that so depicted her personality to all who knew her, and she began to tell me that she had met Abraham, Moses, and Gideon. She went on to tell me how amazing heaven was and that she could see Jesus sitting on the throne and how amazingly beautiful everything was. She described the angels and the living creatures and said that they were mind-blowingly cool. She also mentioned some of her relatives who she had seen only once or twice while they were alive on earth. All of a sudden the smile gave way to sadness as her head began to droop, and then her head lifted as she looked right at me and said, "But I wasn't meant to be here yet. I wasn't meant to be here right now."

I awoke with my heart pounding in my chest. It was like I could feel exactly what she was feeling and understood why she was sad in such a happy place. She was in heaven, not in hell, that was for sure; however, I felt that the sadness on her face came from the fact that she had a call of God upon her life, a destiny to fulfill here on earth that was now gone from her grasp. For all eternity she would live with the knowledge that she had something mighty set aside for her time on earth, but now she would be unable to fulfill it.

I shared this story at the funeral as people wept, reassuring them that I felt this was a dream from God to say that this young lady was not taken, but was definitely received. Jesus died for all our sins, even the ones we haven't repented of or are not even aware of. Jesus died not to send people to hell but to rescue them from hell and get them into heaven!

Prayer is the key to receiving answers from heaven when earth's mortality is at a loss for words. Prayer invades the impossible. Prayer changes the unchangeable.

I saw God heal a little boy with an inoperable tumor by shrinking it overnight after I prayed for him. I saw a little boy who was diagnosed deaf get completely healed when prayer was made, and today he has perfect hearing. A woman who had nine miscarriages and was told she would never be able to carry a fetus all the way to full term now has two babies. God *loves* to perform miracles. He just longs for believers to create an environment of faith.

Many years ago when I was a youth pastor in New Zealand, I was standing in our pre-service prayer meeting on a Saturday night when I felt an overwhelming sense that we needed to pray for lost people. As we began to cry out, I felt to pray against the spirit of suicide that had gripped the island nation of New Zealand, who at that time had the highest rate of teen suicide in the world. Prayer became incredibly intense and forceful, focused, but certainly not undemonstrative. This prayer meeting normally lasted for ten minutes max, and getting people to participate was like pulling teeth. However, this was almost twenty minutes in, and the noise of so many young people engaged told me it wasn't abating and it remained at fever pitch for another quarter of an hour. I had to call a halt because our youth group was about to start and we were the leaders who were meant to start it.

Our church building was located on an industrial street that was completely deserted on a Saturday evening, allowing us to have zero noise complaints as our band thumped out praise and worship at 110 decibels. About halfway through the night a young man walked into the building, looking somewhat bewildered, and stood on the edge of the back row looking around as though he was making sure he could locate all the exits to make a quick getaway should the need present itself. I was meant to be speaking on relationships that evening but found myself speaking about the dangers of the occult, the power of suicide, and child abuse. Every time I tried to get back on point, I would feel an intense burden to go back to the occult, suicide, and abuse. When the time came for the altar call, the young man sitting in the back raised his hand, and with some assistance came forward, surrendering his life to Christ.

He told us that he had no idea what was happening or who we were. He had no idea that we were a youth group and had had no intention of going to church that evening. He had actually left his home to end his life by throwing himself off a bridge about two kilometers away. He had experienced so much tragedy in his life: divorce, abuse, bullying, and massive rejection. In desperation he had turned to the occult in an attempt to get some power over those who had hurt him so badly, but when nothing came, he decided to end his life. He left his home that evening to throw himself off the bridge and become another statistic in New Zealand's teen suicide epidemic. However, he said that as he was walking a voice said to him, *Turn left here!* Puzzled, he thought he could give himself a few extra minutes to investigate before committing to what was to him the inevitable. As he turned down the street, he came to another street where once again the voice spoke and said, *Go down this street!* He could hear music and the voice said, *Go to the music!* He followed it down to our building and walked inside. And instead of committing suicide that evening, he gave his life to God and was powerfully delivered from the demonic influence that had gripped his life. I believe that it was "tarrying" in prayer that enabled God to send angels to rescue him out of the grip of these demons of suicide.

There are demonic forces at play. The Bible makes this clear. Prayer is the way we get involved and tip the scales to favor God's will. Prayer changes the outcome. Without prayer the devil too often inflicts his will of destruction upon our lives. To believe that God is the author of every suicide, death, and murder, or of little kids drowning in backyard swimming pools, requires one to resolve that God Himself is not all good. The sad story I told in the introduction of this book about the little child on life support whose parents believed that it was God's will to take their child for His "glory" continues to grieve me to this day.

God did not *take* him, but God definitely *received* him! There is a huge difference! One is an act of cold, calculated indifference, and the other an act of wondrous grace! God is not in the habit of killing children and taking them for selfish, unexplained, or mysterious reasons. These are the things that happen in a world that has made it bluntly clear, "Not Thy will, but my will be done!" Remember, we live in a fallen world, but it is fallen because we have chosen our own path and not God's. Therefore, we live in a world plagued by pain, sadness, disappointment, tragedy, and even death. God did *not* take the child by orchestrating his death in a backyard pond at age three, but God did lovingly receive the little guy into eternity where he will be reunited with his mother and father and there will be no more tears and no more pain (or drowning for that matter).

This is the hope that we have as believers in Jesus Christ, who conquered death and hell. While it may appease some folks to believe that this was God's perfect will and therefore His doing, I am sorry to say that this does not line up with the Scriptures and neither is it consistent with God's character. We live in a world that has rejected the lordship of its Creator, and each and every moment of each and every day we struggle with putting our will under His will. Man has been given the will to choose, and each day we suffer many consequences of not only our own choices but also the choices of others. Think Columbine, the Pentagon and the World Trade Center on 9/11, the Fort Hood massacre, and drunk drivers who ignore the law and take innocent lives who happen to be traveling on the same stretch of road that evening.

Because God is not a despot, He does not violate our free will or rule by force and coercion. God intervenes in the affairs of men when we cry out to Him in prayer or via an intercessor. This is because the very presence of free will *demands* that there can be no interference. Otherwise, how can it be free will? When we pray, we are inviting God to come and intervene in our affairs. Jesus, in the book of Revelation (3:20), says, "Behold, I stand at the door and knock. If anyone hears My voice and opens the door, I will come in to him and dine with him, and he with Me." Notice Jesus doesn't just burst in, nor does He knock the door down. He stands there politely, respecting your turf, and waits to be responded to and invited inside.

The second way God intervenes is through the entrance of His Word into the earth.

> Then the LORD saw it, and it displeased Him that there was no justice. He saw that there was no man, and wondered that there was no intercessor; therefore His own arm brought salvation for Him; and His own righteousness, it sustained Him (Isa. 59:15–16).

Because all have sinned and fall short of the glory of God, and "there is none righteous, no, not one; there is none who understands; there is none who seeks after God. They have all turned aside" (Rom. 3:10–12). Man left unto himself degenerates into nothing more than a reprobate. So God sends His Word into the earth so that He is able to intervene on the basis of His keeping His word as a God of truth, one who cannot lie.

Surely the Sovereign LORD does nothing without revealing his plan to his servants the prophets. (Amos 3:7 NIV)

The servants of God are the prophets who speak forth His Word into the earth. God being a God of truth is now enabled to perform His Word because it is in keeping with truth. God is faithful to watch over His Word to perform it; He is not a man that He should lie (Jer. 1:12, Num. 23:19). Intercession and the Word of God released into the earth are the two ways that God intervenes in the affairs of men.

Satan is the accuser of the brethren. He is also an accuser of God. The opening chapters of Job reveal this. For God to move sovereignly in the earth would be seen as thuggery by the devil, God forcing His way against the free will and free reign of the inhabitants of the earth. This would be a violation of the authorities and jurisdictions that He has set in place.

For through him God created everything in the heavenly realms and on earth. He made the things we can see and the things we can't see—such as thrones, kingdoms, rulers, and authorities in the unseen world. Everything was created through him and for him. (Col. 1:16 NLT)

God has set these thrones and dominions in place; however, what God has not set in place is *who* sits on them. These are up for grabs. The book of Proverbs teaches that it's the wickedness of a land that seats many princes over that land.

By the transgression of a land many are its princes, but by a man of understanding and knowledge, so it endures. (Prov. 28:2 NASB)

This is how the kingdom of heaven operates. God first looks for an intercessor who makes it his or her will to prefer God's will and pray it into our terra firma! Failing that, God then reveals His will to His servants the prophets who "speak forth" His Word into the atmosphere of the earth so that God who "watches over His word" has jurisdiction to perform it, since it was spoken by one who had been given authority in the earth. God is an invitation God, not a thug or a bully, but a perfect gentlemen. But make no mistake He is beyond smart and has already won the victory countering every move both mankind and principalities make. He is just that awesome!

On a Lighter Note

A favorite comedy routine I like to do is that of the paradoxes of aviation safety. There's so much material to draw from when you're sitting in a hollow metal tube with wings, flying at an altitude of 35,000 feet at speeds in excess of 450 miles per hour. My favorite line, one that usually draws a lot of laughs, is, "Someone told me to relax, that the plane isn't going to go down and you ain't gonna die until it's your turn." I then pause for effect, look somewhat bewildered, and ask—"But what if it's the pilot's turn? If it's his turn, we are all stuffed!"

The comedy plays upon the presupposition that there is a time and day appointed for our death that we have no voice or control over. It's set in stone, determined before time began. Everything is preordained by God; we are just helpless little pawns in a giant game of chess with a predetermined outcome. But the Bible does not endorse such a position. Not only did God endow us with a free will to make choices, but these choices have a massive effect upon our lives and carry certain outcomes. Many believe that everything that happens is God's will. Well, what if not everything is God's perfect will? What if . . .

Some believe that life is like a game of chess with God predetermining the moves, with us being the pieces, absent of any will to make choices or move apart from what He has set and predetermined. We simply sit idly by awaiting His use to bring Himself glory. But the Bible teaches a slightly different perspective on this cosmic game of chess. It teaches that God knows the end of a thing from the beginning (Isa. 46:10), is omniscient (all-knowing), and so brilliant that He is able to bring about His will with each and every piece having free will to move because being beyond any chess-master we know of, He is able to work with each and every decision we make, and is able to make "all things work together for good" (Rom. 8:28).

The first reduces God to one unable to work with the free will of man and therefore must remove it. The second places God as so brilliant that He is able to bring His will to pass *despite* the exercise of man's free will.

All-Knowing, All-Powerful, All-Present, and All-Willing Too?

Some Christians prefer to believe that everything that happens is God's perfect will, a kind of theological ignorance, a perpetual state of bliss/denial believing there is truth in the old adage "ignorance is bliss." To these folks, if anything happens "it was meant to happen," and God has it all under control; therefore, they don't need to take any responsibility or worry about it.

Er, although now that you mention it, I just hope God isn't thinking too much about me right now and wanting to teach me something through suffering with cancer or something random like that. I'll just live at a distance . . . I still like Him and all, and I'll continue to give Him my worship, but I don't want to get too close . . .

If that thought has crossed your mind or frequents the highway synapses of your brain on a regular basis, then be set free! Too many people live in a terrible state of fear when it comes to God, believing His will is unknowable, not to mention unpredictable, and random without respect of their desires and passions in life. If God is the author of both good and evil and wills everything to happen, then the best scenario is not closeness or intimacy with God, because He may well choose my suffering to bring Him glory without the courtesy of an explanation. After all, He is God.

The Bible does not teach that God is "all-willing." It does teach that God is omniscient (all-knowing), omnipresent (everywhere at once), and omnipotent (all-powerful). But nowhere does the Bible teach that God is all-willing. To say that God is all-willing places one in a precarious position theologically, especially when we are trying to grapple with issues like the origin of sin and why God put the blinkin' tree in the garden in the first place if He *knew* that Adam and Eve would eat from it! It introduces us to thoughts and concepts of the character of God being less than holy, perhaps even sinister. Like a God who has stated that He is holy and pure, but like our earthly experience, things are never as good as they seem. Our deepest fears stir within us that perhaps God has an evil streak or a dark side to Him, much like the concept of Eastern yin and yang indicating a little good in evil and a little evil in good.

God is not the author of death. He is the author of life! God is the vanquisher of death; He is *not* the author of it. You will have an impossible time trying to prove from the Scriptures that God is the author of death. Death came as a result of sin. Sin came as a result of rebellion against God. Rebellion against God came as a result of pride in Lucifer's heart. God did *not* create Lucifer's heart with rebellious, self-exalting pride. He created Lucifer to worship, and that meant exercising his will to do so. Lucifer decided he no longer wished to worship but rather wished to be worshiped. But God is God because He alone has the character to sustain being worshiped. Lucifer's vanity began the downward spiral and his impending doom is inevitable.

EIGHT

Battlefield Earth

*Delight yourself also in the Lord, and He
shall give you the desires of your heart.*
—PSALM 37:4

"Guess what?" shrieked my wife excitedly as she burst through the door. Before I could answer, she blurted out, "I had lunch with someone today who told me she has had three dreams that I am pregnant!"

My very centered and balanced reply was, "There's no way you're pregnant; that's crazy!" (Deep down, though, I had been hoping for a number of years for a daughter to complete the family "quiver," so to speak.) *Could this really be it?*

God had encouraged me that He was going to give me a daughter. Just six months earlier we received news from Australia that my mother was dying, and with us being halfway round the world in San Diego busy in church-planting work, there was little we could do other than pray. Early one morning I could not sleep because of the hopelessness I felt for my mother. It was shortly after 4:00 a.m. so I decided to get up and pray. The heavy

Californian marine layer cloaked the path where I walked like a thick fog, making it difficult to see any farther ahead than about twenty feet. It was cold, wet, and dark, much like the hopelessness I was feeling so far away from my mother. Then as clear as I have ever heard God speak to me, He said, *I'm going to give you a daughter, and she will comfort you in the loss of your mother.* I was so shocked and surprised at the same time. Flabbergasted, I just stopped walking and lifted my hands to heaven, surrendering and graciously accepting the goodness of God. I have found that God is just so beautiful that He does things He doesn't need to simply because He is good. His faithfulness and loving-kindness toward us take my breath away again and again.

The problem was, I couldn't really tell my wife, Leanne. We already had three boys at home and Leanne was convinced that I could not *make* girls, only boys. So the subject of trying for a fourth child meant risking having four boys. Our three sons often engaged in testosterone-fueled scrapping, fighting, and tag team wrestling that turned our living room into an octagon, damaging the furniture, walls, and appliances. Adding to this stress for my wife was not a suggestion I particularly wanted to bring up. Not right then anyway.

Leanne had gone down to the CVS pharmacy that day and purchased three pregnancy tests, all of which confirmed that she was indeed pregnant. Now that it was too late to change the diagnosis, I told her that God had spoken to me months earlier that He was giving us a daughter who would comfort me in the loss of my mother. Leanne gave me that "Are you serious?" look, but it had been a strange day already: we were not planning on having another baby, but a divine hand seemed to be at play, so she just smiled, accepting what I had spoken. Zoe Abigail Sigrid Matthesius was coming to join the clan and complete the quiver and I was as excited as Augustus Gloop in a donut store! Was this God's will? You better believe it. God's will is His Word, and His Word is His will. How do I know what God's will is? If it's in His Word then it's in His will! "Delight yourself also in the LORD, and He shall give you the desires of your heart" (Ps. 37:4). I had left all and followed the call to serve Jesus and His purposes for my life, counting the cost again and again, and here was God reminding me that living for Him is a two-way street. You delight in Him and put Him first and He certainly will bring those desires that you have bubbling in your heart into a reality. Be willing to pay whatever price is necessary to please Him. Go on, I dare you!

A Baby Is Not Born Without Some PUSH Taking Place!

You cannot live a life of devotion and wholehearted service to the Lord and *not* find yourself the beneficiary of incredible blessings, favor, goodness, and abundance! Twenty weeks into the pregnancy we received our confirmation during the ultrasound that the baby inside of Leanne's tummy was indeed a little baby girl! Tears of elation coursed down our cheeks as we praised God for His loving-kindness. Then, almost instantly the joy was sucked out of the room like a bird getting sucked into the jet engine of a plane. The nurse let fly a chorus of "Oh no, that's not good" as the joy turned into concern and joy left the room as fear entered in. They asked us to come back for a second ultrasound, a much more in-depth one, urging it was very necessary as there were some serious concerns they had regarding the health of our little baby girl. They used words like "Down syndrome," "chromosome deficiencies," and "developmental issues," all of which seemed to strike a permanent blow to the goodness of God and His benevolent gift to us.

The car ride home from the hospital felt like forever as Leanne quizzed me as to why God would do such a thing. "Why would He give us a child with special needs? Doesn't He think that our lives are busy and stressful enough?" I sat silent for the longest time, then said: "I don't think God is, sweetheart!"

When we got home Leanne went up to our bedroom to escape being probed by a barrage of questions from the inquisitive minds of our sons. Meanwhile, I went into our spare room, pulled out my guitar, and began to worship God, trying to get some answers or at least some peace. I had been worshiping for a good half hour or so when I finally felt strong enough to pray. *What's going on, God? Speak to me. If this is Your will let me know, and if not, speak to me and tell me what to do!*

I felt strongly in my spirit that this was the enemy trying to steal our joy and rob us of a wonderful testimony of God's goodness and blessing. He is always trying to make God look bad. He started it in Eden and he has not relented since. Then I felt the Lord whisper a scripture to me. I'd love to say I was familiar with it and could recall it immediately, but no, I had to go look it up.

The verse was James 1:17. Upon opening my Bible and turning to the passage, I read these words: "Every good gift and every perfect gift is from above, and comes down from the Father of lights, with whom there is no variation or shadow of turning." I immediately felt the Spirit say, *What I have given you is good and perfect; this is the spoiler trying to spoil what I have given you!*

I knew the devil was using more than just discouragement to rob us of the joy and blessing God was bringing into our lives. So many times I thought to myself, *Why can't this just be an easy, normal deal like other people go through?* But before I could finish the thought, I knew why we were going through it. We were meant to overcome and turn the test into a testimony!

Every night and every day we prayed James 1:17. We spoke *over* the top of the doctors' reports and the various diagnoses given us, and today we have a magnificent, completely healthy, unbelievably intelligent little daughter called Zoe Abigail (meaning "life" and "father's delight"), who is the crown of our family and a trophy of the grace and goodness of God.

God knew the enemy was trying to steal our joy, but He made it abundantly clear that *His will* was for us to have a beautiful, healthy daughter. We had to understand that there was also a powerful force at work trying to do all in his power to make sure we did not become recipients of God's perfect will and intentions. This is what the Bible describes as "spiritual warfare," and it's why we need to understand our authority as believers as well as how powerful the Word of God is. There is nothing more powerful in the universe. It turns darkness into light, chaos into order, and death into life!

Knowing Is Not Willing

Was it God's will for Adam and Eve to disobey Him and eat from the tree of the knowledge of good and evil? Of course not; how could God be the author or director of disobedience? Did God *know* that they were going to? The Scriptures seem to indicate that God foreknew the choice that Adam and Eve would make, because the Bible says that Jesus was the Lamb that was slain "from the foundation of the world" (Rev. 13:8).

God may *know* all things, but that does not mean that God *causes* all things or *wills* all things! You and I have been given free will, the power to choose our own way, and therefore we live in a world that sees man's will dominating the landscape of human affairs and atrocities. Adolf Hitler was deceived and deluded to believe that he was doing the will of God by exterminating the Jewish race. We know which spirit spoke to him to wipe out God's chosen people—it certainly was not the Spirit of God. Hitler chose with his own free will to believe a lie and in turn wrought one of the greatest human atrocities of the twentieth century.

If God Knows, Then Why Doesn't He Prevent?

This is probably the most frequently asked question by apostates (people who have fallen away from faith in God). I was watching Joel Osteen being grilled on CNN by one of its key anchors over the question, "If there is a God, and especially one who claims to be loving, how could He allow things like the Holocaust to happen?"

The anchor then spoke about how his grandmother gave up on her faith because she went through the horrors of the Holocaust and Nazi Germany. "How can you say that there is a loving God when things like that happen?" was the question asked of the man often dubbed by the media as "America's favorite pastor."

God certainly is all-knowing, but does this mean that God knows every evil thing that a person will do, or worse yet, predestines people to commit evil? Should God's job be to intervene to halt all the evil that men desire to commit? Many agnostics and atheists feel as though they can justify their lack of faith in God based upon a supposition of a poor performance scorecard by the divine potentate! They feel that while there is evil in the world and men committing heinous crimes and often getting away with them, they have a defensible position on not having to give any devotion or homage to God, because He should have intervened in the evils these men wanted to commit (as long as He doesn't interfere with the evils they want to commit).

God, the Divine Referee?

Is God's job description "Divine Referee"? To always halt any acts of evil anytime and every time they are about to happen? This theme is the subject matter in the movie *Minority Report*, a futuristic sci-fi police force thriller starring Tom Cruise, where three psychic siblings solve crimes before they are ever committed. The department is called "pre-crime," and three psychic albinos have their brain activity—or specifically the imagery of their dreams—hooked up to a super computer that interprets the data and immediately sends its findings to the "pre-crime" lab. The lab sends out its police officers to arrest the perpetrator before he or she commits the crime. That is until our albino siblings reveal the next crime to be committed is by none other than the leading police officer, played by Tom Cruise. It really ramps up from there!

Ten-Yard Penalty?

Many people believe that it is God's job to referee the world and keep everything safe and serene for everyone. However, wouldn't it be considered "unjust" if every time a person desired to exercise his or her free will, God intervened and blocked him or her from doing so unless it was exactly what He wanted? God has given man free will, and it wouldn't be free if there were interference and controlling forces from the giver of the gift. Remember, free will has an extraordinary price tag attached to it. God chose to implement a plan where His only begotten Son came to earth to be crucified, rather than have no free will for man at all. Man has the ability to choose good or evil. God desires with all His heart that we choose good, knowing that we are not so much punished *for* our sins as we are punished *by* our sins. "The wages of sin is death" (Rom. 6:23).

Let me explain. Most would concede that even though hijackers desired to crash a commercial airplane into the Capitol in Washington, DC, that would *not* be God's perfect will for those people involved. God's perfect will would be something along the lines of the hijackers coming to repentance, getting saved, and everyone landing safely singing songs like "Great Is Our God"! Then the peace resulting from the newfound friendship would spill over and bring peace in the Middle East (or something along these lines). Yet every day we see, hear, and experience less than God's best or God's will for our lives, and sadly every day we are exposed in some way or another to all kinds of evil, usually by way of crime or tragedy.

Free but Expensive

You and I have the power to choose what we will do, all day and every day! God's gift of free will can only exist if He Himself will not violate it. Otherwise it is not free!

The flaw of Calvinism is that it reduces us to pre-programmed robots performing God's will like pawns on a chessboard. Can you imagine how immature it would be if two people were playing chess, and upon the completion of the game the loser takes half of the pawns off the table, walks over to the fireplace, and says, "That's it! You're burning in the fire—you lost me the game with those stupid moves!" It had nothing to do with the pieces on the board and everything to do with the one controlling the pieces. Yet this is not dissimilar to the position of extreme Calvinists, who believe that everything that happens is God's will, denying the existence of free will and in turn making God look like a tantrum-throwing chess match loser. Crazy!

If everything that happens in this life is because God willed it to happen, then how can He judge us for our choices? They were the choices He decided we should choose and, therefore, we are an arbitrary player in the grand scheme of things and thereby innocent, as we are unable to resist against the Almighty and His will! However, the Bible is very clear that God is completely just and completely righteous and has therefore given us a free will to choose, informing us that we will be judged based upon the choices of our free will.

A Hell of a Question

Probably one of the most difficult questions one of my children has ever asked me was, "If God knows who will go to heaven and who will go to hell, why doesn't He stop those people who are going to choose hell from being born in the first place?" Man, what a question! What was at stake in my son's mind was the justness of God. If God was indeed good and hell was so bad, why wouldn't He be so merciful as to stop those people from being born in the first place so that everyone would go to heaven and no one would suffer in hell?

God has made sure that nobody needs to go to hell. Jesus died for the sins of the whole world, not just the righteous. However, God, being just, will not stop people from having what they want. If they do not want God, if they want nothing to do with Him or His purposes in their lives, then God graciously gives them exactly what they ask for—a place where He isn't.

Unfortunately that is the place we have come to call hell. It is the place that the God of the Bible repeatedly warns us against. Much like driving on a freeway and ignoring the signs that say

Wrong Way, you keep driving and then want to blame the department of main roads for your head-on collision with a truck!

God is the source of all life, the fountain of love, light, and all that is called good. So to be completely removed from God is to be completely removed from life, light, love, goodness, and joy. Psalm 16:11 says, "In Your presence is fullness of joy." All of these things belong exclusively to God. Hell is the place where God has purposely removed His presence, so there is no joy, no justice, no peace, no light, no love, and no comfort. In fact, in this vacuum the exact opposite prevails. Trust me, you do not want to go to this place, and you want to do whatever you can to warn people about going there!

There is evil in the world not because God desires it or even wills it. Evil exists because there are beings that desire to do evil and possess the power to do so. It began with Lucifer's rebellion in heaven, then it spread virally, infecting one third of the angels of heaven. It did not stop there but permeated all the way down through creation.

God has appointed a Judgment Day to bring closure to the evil residents in the universe. Man was created in God's image and likeness, but there are two forces or influences at play in our universe: Lucifer's contagion and God's righteousness. Men have chosen to do evil even though God is continually willing and desiring them to choose right, do good, and choose life! One requires preferring and pleasing God over self; the other just prefers and pleases self. God does not will for there to be evil, but He does permit it to be so. However, like an outbreak of a deadly plague, He has already contained it, defeated it, destroyed and removed it by placing it into time where He has placed an expiration date upon it.

This was accomplished through the Lamb of God slain from the foundation of the world. I'm not sure if you knew this, but to create an antidote to the poisonous venom of a snake, physicians would have a lamb bitten by the serpent, then the blood of that lamb containing powerful antibodies would be used to create anti-venom or an antidote to the serpent's poison. Sound familiar? This is what God did through Jesus Christ. However, the choice remains with each one of us to choose whom we serve.

The great Old Testament leader Joshua zeroed in on this when he brought a powerful challenge to the nation of Israel:

> And if it seems evil to you to serve the LORD, choose for yourselves this day whom you will serve, whether the gods which your fathers served that were on the other side of the River, or the gods of the Amorites, in whose land you dwell. But as for me and my house, we will serve the LORD. (Josh. 24:15)

If God Is Good, Then Why?

The default position for people who do not want to commit their lives to God is, "Let's blame God for all the suffering in the world!" After all, if God is indeed good (and He most certainly is), then how come bad things happen to good people? In fact, why do bad things happen at all?

Albert Einstein said, "The mathematical precision of the universe reveals the mathematical mind of God."[1] One of the most magnificent scientific minds of the ages figured out from observing the mathematical precision and wonder of the universe that there was without a doubt a designer or creator who authored and put all things together. He knew this ordered universe could not have come together by random chance or accidental cosmic chain reactions—it was guided, ordered, and structured perfectly by what can only be a perfect being, or God. Einstein went on to say, "A knowledge of the existence of something we cannot penetrate, of the manifestations of the profoundest reason and the most radiant beauty—it is this knowledge and this emotion that constitute the truly religious attitude; in this sense, and in this alone, I am a deeply religious man."[2]

However, a great dilemma existed within Einstein. The God whose signature he clearly saw in the order of the universe was not the same God the church of his day spoke of—a God who "allowed" children to be born deformed and who "allowed" rapists and pedophiles to evade justice and remain at large. The theology of his day was very much that of a Calvinistic strain, and therefore decreed that everything that happened in the world must be the will of God. The difference between the God of the universe and the God who causes and "wills" imperfections and injustices to exist in human beings was too much for Einstein to accept—that this could be one and the same God.[3]

Einstein's Error

What the theology of Einstein's day did not and would not accept was that Satan is not only the author of evil, but also the god of this age (2 Cor. 4:4).[4] As I have already mentioned, Jesus called him the "ruler of this world" (John 12:31). Because of this very present evil, corruption has set itself into every facet of our existence and permeated itself into every area of our world. Einstein was only seeing the mathematical precision of the universe, proving indeed that there must be a divine being—God—who created all things; however, an ignorance of what truths are revealed within the Scriptures caused him to miss seeing that this was the same God spoken of throughout the pages of the Bible.

The Bible does not hide the fact that this world is fraught with pain, suffering, and evil. In fact, the Scriptures go to great lengths to explain not only their origins but also their remedies, namely that God will triumph over all of this and finally put an end to pain, suffering, and wickedness along with its authors and purveyors.

The time will come when God's perfect will will ultimately triumph, and we will live as God originally intended us to live: in perfect peace and harmony and in perfect communion with Him and with each other. We are caught in a moment of unfolding chronology. The Bible refers to this as "time." Because of God's perfect righteousness, He must allow these forces to play out and have their full expression until all is completely resolved at the Day of Judgment, wherein time, sin, and death will be no more.

The perfect will of God for our lives *can* be and *must* be arbitrarily activated in our lives. God's promises give us victory in all things, but make no mistake, God's will does not automatically happen just because God wants it to happen. In fact, God's will cannot happen in our lives until it goes through a metamorphosis and becomes our will!

NINE

Battle Royale

God's cause is committed to men; God commits
Himself to men. Praying men are the vice-regents
of God; they do His work and carry out His plans.
—E. M. BOUNDS

Jesus instructed us both by His teaching and by His example that the will of God comes to pass in our lives through the conduit of prayer. He did this when He knelt in the Garden of Gethsemane and prayed, "Father, if it is possible, let this cup pass from Me; nevertheless, not as I will, but as You will" (Matt. 26:39). Or when He taught the disciples to pray what has today become known in many Catholic circles as the "Our Father" instructing us that the purpose of prayer begins with worship, then moves into mission: "Thy Kingdom come, Thy will be done on earth as it is in heaven . . ." Those who elevate the teaching of men above the truths of the holy Scriptures would have you believe that we are not engaged in a battle of wills and that God's will is happening all the time, everywhere, in everything because He is sovereign. I know we have already dismantled this spurious teaching, but let me show you another powerful story found in the gospels of Jesus Christ to drive this point home!

> Then Jesus went out from there and departed to the region of Tyre and Sidon. And behold, a woman of Canaan came from that region and cried out to Him, saying, "Have mercy on me, O Lord, Son of David! My daughter is severely demon-possessed." But He answered her not a word. And His disciples came and urged Him, saying, "Send her away, for she cries out after us." But He answered and said, "I was not sent except to the lost sheep of the house of Israel." Then she came and worshiped Him, saying, "Lord, help me!" But He answered and said, "It is not good to take the children's bread and throw it to the little dogs." And she said, "Yes, Lord, yet even the little dogs eat the crumbs which fall from their masters' table." Then Jesus answered and said to her, "O woman, great is your faith! Let it be to you as you desire." And her daughter was healed from that very hour. (Matt. 15:21–28)

There are three distinct elements in this passage of Scripture. First, she was praying to the right God. If you want your prayers to get answered, superstition and ritual will not suffice, but praying to Jesus—the "Son of David," the Messiah—is the first step. But from there the story took an unpropitious turn. Jesus ignored her. He didn't even bother to give her a no! This was made worse by the disciples shooing her away to echo the fact that it seemed Jesus was completely indifferent to her plight and the suffering of her daughter at the hands of the devil.

Second, after realizing she would not leave quietly, Jesus let her know that He "was not sent except to the lost sheep of the house of Israel" and she was *not* one of those. She was a Canaanite woman and therefore outside of the covenant God had made with Abraham and his descendants. There was no deliverance for her in this covenant because she was a Gentile. In other words, Jesus was saying to her, "It's not God's will for you—at least at this time." Later the gospel would come to the Gentiles, but not yet.

Third, Jesus then went on to offend her by calling her a dog. He said to her, "It is not good to take the children's bread and throw it to the little dogs." You would think this would have been enough to dissuade her from any further inquiry. Jesus had offended her. People have left churches for much less than being called a dog. Yet her persistence prevailed when she said, "Yes, Lord, yet even the little dogs eat the crumbs which fall from their masters' table!" At this Jesus was so impressed by her faith that she received exactly what she came for, despite her Canaanite background and exclusion from the covenants of Israel. Had she quit, her daughter would have remained vexed by the devil. Had she gotten offended or accepted the theological position presented to her that she was not included in Israel's blessing of the Messiah's visit, her daughter would have remained tormented by the devil.

Yet the story does not end this way—she overcame three obstacles and secured a miracle for her daughter. There are three lessons we can learn from this mother when it comes to prayer:

1. Persistence overcomes resistance. There is always
   a level of resistance that exists in prayers being answered,

and persistence is the antidote (also see Luke 18, the parable of the persistent widow).

2. **Worship woos God's heart.** God is drawn toward those who worship. The Scriptures show again and again that praise and worship precede breakthrough. Most folks worship once something good happens, but this woman knelt and worshiped while heaven was silent and indifferent to her suffering.

3. **Faith is tenacious.** Faith persists when heaven resists, it worships when the answer is delayed or seemingly denied, and it understands that there is more power in one crumb that falls from the Master's table than all the institutions of man put together.

What Causes This Resistance?

As believers we are told to arm ourselves for conflict. There is a battle raging, but the apostle Paul makes it clear in Ephesians 6 that it is not with men that we war. Our issue is not with humanity, but with principalities, thrones, dominions, authorities, and the spiritual hosts of wickedness in the heavenly places.

We are called to war in this realm because it is here that the battles are won and lost. When a pastor admits his city is a tough city, he has already yielded ground to the enemy and given up his position of power in the city. Put on the armor of God and go to battle in the heavenly realms by speaking the Word of God into it, and you can change the atmosphere that is shaping your city. In the

Scriptures angels come from the heavenly realm into the earth for *no other* reason than to bring God's Word into it. This is because God's Word shapes, changes, and realigns the world to His will.

The fiercest opposition to the will of God is in the heavenly places. Here satanic forces array themselves against God, influencing mankind to continually rebel against the perfect will of God, to make the sons and daughters of men become objects of God's wrath and judgment. What Satan achieved in the garden of Eden, he has set up on a massive global scale in the heavenly places over our cities, deceiving men with, "Has God really said?" and "Go your own way, do your own thing, don't trust God; He is holding out on you, limiting your experience and pleasure; you can be just like Him, knowing good and evil!" The battle rages, and it is a battle of wills.

The Battle Is Internal and External

For what I am doing, I do not understand. For what I will to do, that I do not practice; but what I hate, that I do. If, then, I do what I will not to do, I agree with the law that it is good. But now, it is no longer I who do it, but sin that dwells in me. For I know that in me (that is, in my flesh) nothing good dwells; for to will is present with me, but how to perform what is good I do not find. For the good that I will to do, I do not do; but the evil I will not to do, that I practice. Now if I do what I will not to do, it is no longer I who do it, but sin that dwells in me.

I find then a law, that evil is present with me, the one who wills to do good. For I delight in the law of God according to the inward man. But I see another law in my members, warring against the law of my mind, and bringing me into captivity to the law of sin which is in my members. O wretched man that I am! Who will deliver me from this body of death? I thank God—through Jesus Christ our Lord! (Rom. 7:15–25)

We have all seen the struggling momma in the supermarket with the three-year-old in the checkout line wanting some candy. She tells him no, and he throws himself into a rage that resembles something from the movie *The Exorcist*. The mother looks into the faces of the surrounding onlookers, desperately trying to avoid eye contact with the judgmental crew who are already muttering what a terrible parent she must be, and she proclaims, "He's just so strong-willed!" God has seven billion people He's parenting, and you and I are two of them.

How powerful is the human will? Dr. Phil Pringle says, "Not even God will violate what He has set in place. If you resist God, He will resist you. If you draw near to God, He will draw near to you. If you resist the devil, he will flee from you. These are all engagements of *your will* and dramatically affect your life!"

The power of the human will, sometimes referred to as the human spirit, is regularly quoted in various fields of human enterprise where bravery, courage, and overcoming insurmountable odds take place. However, can this human will or human spirit that helps human beings to triumph and succeed also work against God? Can the human will work independent of God and be directed and focused upon personal gain at God's expense? Or when employed (yielded and surrendered), can it produce kingdom-building results for God?

Self-will Trumps God's Will

I know what you're thinking: *blasphemy!* Well, hear me out.

The Bible teaches us that the human will is so powerful that if we resist the devil he will flee from us and if we reject God He will reject us, but if we will draw near to God then He will draw near to us (James 4:7–8). Yes, the human will is just that powerful! You can, with your will, choose to push God away or you can draw near to Him and have Him therefore draw near to you, thus experiencing His presence and goodness. These are all acts of your will.

Look at David's references to his will in Psalm 101:1–8:

> I will sing of mercy and justice; to You, O LORD, I will sing praises. I will behave wisely in a perfect way. Oh, when will You come to me? I will walk within my house with a perfect heart. I will set nothing wicked before my eyes; I hate the work of those who fall away; it shall not cling to me. A perverse heart shall depart from me; I will not know wickedness. Whoever secretly slanders his neighbor, Him I will destroy; the one who has a haughty look and a proud heart, Him I will not endure. My eyes shall be on the faithful of the land, that they may dwell with me; he who walks in a perfect way, he shall serve me. He who works deceit shall not dwell within my house; he who tells lies shall not continue in my presence. Early I will destroy all the wicked of the land, that I may cut off all the evildoers from the city of the LORD.

Nine times David says "I will," determining that his will was aligning itself or at least embracing God's will as his highest purpose.

"Yes, but I believe that God's will will always override man's will." Okay, let's just say that it is God's will for you to go to a great city and preach but you decide you don't want to go; you want to party in another city instead. Would God override your will, or would you be able to go wherever you like?

Welcome to the story of Jonah. God's will for Jonah came to him by the "word of the Lord" (God's will is *always* congruent with His Word), and it was for Jonah to "Arise, go to Nineveh, that great city, and cry out against it!" (Jonah 1:2). Yet Jonah arose and went to Joppa to sail to Tarshish (the exact opposite direction) instead. "Yeah, but Jonah ended up in Nineveh," you say. You may believe, and rightly so, that God's will triumphed in this story. Yes, it did, but only after God helped Jonah change both his attitude and his will. It is amazing what a few days basking in the digestive juices of a fish's belly will do to convince a man that he really ought to rethink his choices and perhaps put God's will above his own.

God did not *force* Jonah to perform His will at the expense of his own; He merely *assisted* Jonah in adjusting his will to make its highest priority the will of God! God's will can only come to pass in your life when you make it *your* will! This is what God seeks above all things in any man or woman who desires to serve Him—a heart that is willing to completely and continually yield to His will above their own. That person is powerful, that person is a threat to the devil, and that person is a channel through which the will of God can come to pass in the earth.

It has been this way throughout both the Bible and history. From Abraham, to Moses, Joshua to Gideon, Joseph, Daniel, and the prophets all the way to Jesus and the disciples, we see God choosing to do mighty exploits through people who are yielded unto Him. A yielded heart is one that forsakes a life of serving and pleasing self and chooses instead to make His will their highest passion, purpose, and calling. This is the greatest quest and pursuit any human being can embrace in this life! Once His will becomes our will, look out! Heaven has found another conduit through which it is able to flow into the world.

God's Intent for Man's Authority and Dominion

In Genesis, God created the heavens and the earth and gave man dominion over the work of His hands. That was His original purpose: "Let Us make man in Our image, according to Our likeness; let them have dominion over the fish of the sea, over the birds of the air, and over the cattle . . ." (Gen. 1:26). God gave man the ability to not only speak but to rule the world by his words. If you look closely, there is a pattern in Genesis. God created through speaking, and then He *called* man to rule over creation. Let me show you: God *said*, "Let there be light," and light was! Then God *called* the light "day," and the darkness He called "night." Then God *said*, "Let there be a firmament," and there was a firmament. Then God *called* it "heaven." Then God *said*, "Let dry land appear," and dry land appeared, and God *called* it "earth."

You see, to create, God "said," but to rule over it, He "called" it. God broke that pattern, however, when He created man. God continued to create by saying, but He stopped calling things when He got to the plants and animals. Instead, He had Adam name those things, from the birds of the air to the beasts of the field and every creeping thing that crept on the ground. Why? Because Adam was to rule over those things. God would rule over the heavens, over the night and the day, over the darkness and the light, but Adam was to rule over the earth and all the things that the Lord God had made.

> Out of the ground the LORD God formed every beast of the field and every bird of the air, and brought them to Adam to see what he would call them. And whatever Adam called each living creature, that was its name. So Adam gave names to all cattle, to the birds of the air, and to every beast of the field. But for Adam there was not found a helper comparable to him. (Gen. 2:19–20)

Adam, meaning "man," was created to rule over the work of God's hands, to have dominion and exercise authority walking in God's light, life, and power. This was robbed from Adam (man) in the garden, through his disobedience of God's commandment in Eden, but it was gloriously restored to us at Calvary through the obedience of the second Adam, Jesus Christ.

The Two Sides of God's Will

On one occasion in the Bible, Jesus was teaching the crowds, and the Pharisees and lawyers—who were threatened by their diminishing audiences as Christ's crowds continued to flourish and grow—asked Him a question designed to trick Him: "Is it lawful to pay taxes to Caesar, or not?" (Matt. 22:17). The religious leaders were spiritually blind and could not see beyond their small paradigm. To them, there was only one will existing in the world, and that was God's will! Therefore, they felt that it was wrong to pay taxes to Caesar. He was not their sovereign; as a nation, Israel was exclusive and exceptional to all other nations—her King was the Lord God Himself. However, saying so publicly was seen by the Romans as treason and would result in being arrested and being subject to the full weight and force of the Roman judiciary. People lived in fear of Roman justice and punishment.

The Pharisees thought that either way they would trap Jesus—either He would be a good Jew and admit that it was outside of God's will to pay taxes to Caesar (they would then notify the Roman authorities and have Jesus arrested as a rebel and insurrectionist), or He would answer and say that it was correct to pay taxes to Caesar, therefore branding Himself a liberal Jew and a compromiser, one who does not hold the statutes and commands taught within the Torah to serve the one God, the Lord! Israel's religious elite had been debating this for years and could not break the stalemate, so they brought it before Jesus, shrewdly believing that they would trap Him and get rid of Him one way or another. The crowds waited with bated breath for his reply.

> But Jesus perceived their wickedness, and said, "Why do you test Me, you hypocrites? Show Me the tax money." So they brought Him a denarius. And He said to them, "Whose image and inscription is this?" They said to Him, "Caesar's." And He said to them, "Render therefore to Caesar the things that are Caesar's, and to God the things that are God's." (Matt. 2:18–21)

There are always two sides of the same coin. As my mother-in-law likes to say, "No matter how flat you make a pancake there's always two sides!" The Bible says that God is "not willing that any should perish" (2 Peter 3:9), and yet people have perished and are perishing even to this day. This is because there are two sides to God's will. There is God's *perfect will* and there is God's *permissible will*. God's *perfect will* is that no one goes to hell, that all accept the immeasurable sacrifice made by His only begotten Son dying on the cross to redeem us with His own blood. However, God has also *permitted* that man has the right to exercise his free will to accept or reject God's free gift and live the way that he likes, even to spit in God's face if he so desires (we see this in the gospels). Therefore, sadly there are people who do perish. It is not His perfect will—it is His reluctant, permissible will.

What this means is that while God is in control, He is not a "control freak." God has *permitted* that men can choose their own way—they can choose to obey Him or choose to disobey Him. They can choose to give life or they can choose like Cain to take life and commit murder.

Doesn't God Know Everything?

Nothing happens without God's knowledge and God's allowing it. But make no mistake, He does not *cause* everything that happens to happen. Contrary to popular belief, God is not the author of every earthquake, flood, murder, rape, or decision. Jesus teaches us in Matthew 7:24–27 that there are people who hear the words of Jesus and choose not to do them (people who build their house on the sand), and then there are people who hear His words and choose to apply them to their lives (builders on the rock). Obviously God's will is that each and every man build his or her life/house on the Rock. Yet God does not override man's ability to choose. Even though it is His will, He does not make it happen—He allows us to exercise our free will and choose!

God *permits* things to happen, but that does not automatically mean that God *purposes* everything to happen. There are things He permits that are secondary to His highest desires, purpose, will, and intent. We see this in the 9/11 tragedy. It is evil to say that that was the work of God or to even hint that it was the desire or will of God! It was the will of man, or in that case men who were consumed by hatred and self-serving religious fervor, believing that their god rewards jihadists and martyrs with seventy virgin brides in exchange for the taking of innocent lives. The Scripture says, "'Vengeance is Mine, I will repay,' says the Lord" (Heb. 10:30). God came to liberate women, not enslave them to more abuse and mistreatment. They are not commodities, nor are they prizes for the person who kills the most "infidels"!

Isn't God's Will Automatic?

Multitudes over the centuries have both pondered and posed questions like, "Is God trying to teach me something through this sickness or tragedy?" and "Why is it that God allows people to suffer?" These questions arise when people see oppression, starvation, cruelty, injustice, murder, death, rape, abuse, and so on.

Pulpits have thundered with the fiery rhetoric of preachers who tell us that the will of God is perfect and just even though we cannot understand it. How dare we question God and why He does what He does! We should just accept all that happens without searching for cause and motive. This is "faith," we are told, and we are called to "live by faith."

But what if the will of God is not automatic? What if the will of God requires not only our participation, but even more than that it requires our "activation" through various spiritual activities like prayer, obedience, and faith? What if the earth we live in is a place where the will of God is being contested every minute of every hour of every day, resulting in the sad reality that God's perfect will rarely happens?

What if I told you that the Scriptures teach that there are both external and internal forces at play that keep the perfect will of God from coming to pass in your life, and in knowing these truths you will not only liberate yourself but be empowered to see God's perfect will come to pass in your life again and again?

Isn't Everything That Happens God's Will?

For if God did not spare the angels who sinned, but cast them down to hell and delivered them into chains of darkness, to be reserved for judgment . . . (2 Peter 2:4)

As we have established already, God does not orchestrate every decision that is made in the universe. Knowledge is entirely separate from program or cause. God cannot be blamed for the rebellion in heaven, and neither is He responsible for every murder, rape, abortion, and crime committed here on the earth. These are the choices of powerful sovereign beings, both human and demonic.

Some believe that God does *whatever* He wants, *whenever* He wants because He is God. They speak these things ignorantly, not knowing that God has bound Himself to both His Word and His laws, which He will not violate. For example, in Ezekiel 22:30 God searched for an intercessor to cry out to Him on behalf of the city (which was steeped in sin and wickedness) so that He might not destroy the city, but sadly He found no one. God wanted to spare the city. He wanted to see salvation come to the city, not judgment and destruction, but because of the righteousness and justice of our God, finding no intercessor, He did not get what He wanted. That was not the first time God did not get what He wanted. In Genesis 6, God was grieved in His heart because the thoughts and intents of man's heart were only evil continually. God did not want that to be the case, but because of another force at work in our universe— namely free will—man had become corrupt and defiled, and so something other than what God wanted prevailed.

Thy Will Be Done on Earth as It Is in Heaven

Then war broke out in heaven. Michael and his angels fought against the dragon, and the dragon and his angels fought back. But he was not strong enough, and they lost their place in heaven. (Rev. 12:7–8 NIV)

It was a beautiful sunny day outside. The kids were off school, and there were many ways we could spend the day in balmy Southern California. After a brief discussion with my wife, Leanne, it was unanimous that we were going to spend the day at the beach. There we would have access to a Starbucks just 500 yards away as well as ice cream and then lunch. We would pack the car with surfboards, body boards, towels, and sunscreen. Oh, what a perfect day at the beach it was going to be.

We gathered the kids together and announced our wonderful plans for the day ahead. We were waiting to be greeted with loud applause and cheers ringing out, statements like, "Yay! You guys are the greatest parents in the whole wide world! Is there anything we can do to help make this joyous event happen?" Reality check. Instead, grumbling and complaining that always seem to accompany these wonderful ideas of ours bombarded us.

"I wanna stay home!" stated my eldest.

"Yeah, why do we have to go to the beach? I wanna play Xbox!" stated my second born.

"You can play Xbox anytime. Today the weather is beautiful, and your mom and I want to have a family day together!" I declared, trying to both reason with them as well as assert my authority.

"Family days suck!" announced our sixteen-year-old. "They are so lame!"

"What's lame about going to the beach?" Leanne piped in with a tone that was less than impressed by our kids' responses.

In our family my will regularly experiences resistance, opposition, and conflict. So, too, does God's will on the earth. In heaven it's a different story now, but even there it has not had a 100 percent perfect record. God has seven billion children here on earth squabbling, fighting, resisting, and sometimes downright rejecting His will on a continual basis. We have an education system that denies His craftsmanship, rejects His ownership, mocks His standards, despises His commandments, and ultimately rejects His authority, preferring instead to be autonomous and accountable to no one. As the psalmist says, "Why do the wicked renounce God? He has said in his heart, 'You will not require an account'" (Ps. 10:13).

Battleground Earth

The earth became the battleground for the will of God. Lucifer, cast down out of heaven, degenerated into the being we now call Satan, who is bent on imposing his will while opposing God's will at all times, resulting in all manner of grief. There are wars and rumors of wars, conflict and oppression, kingdom rising against kingdom, nation against nation, violence, murder, hatred, and all manner of evil because God's will is resisted continuously. The predominant will on the earth has become Satan's, not God's. The Scriptures make this very clear. Let me make a bold statement: man's will and Satan's will dominate and contaminate the earth, while God's perfect will experiences constant resistance and opposition.

> Again, the devil took Him up on an exceedingly high mountain, and showed Him all the kingdoms of the world and their glory. And he said to Him, "All these things I will give You if You will fall down and worship me." Then Jesus said to him, "Away with

you, Satan! For it is written, 'You shall worship the LORD your God, and Him only you shall serve.'" (Matt. 4:8–10)

Satan's longing to be worshiped is revealed in the above verses of Scripture. This is *not* the will of God. Therefore, Satan's relentless quest diametrically opposes, resists, and attacks the perfect will of God to keep it from coming to pass. But God in His omniscience has already calculated all of this, and Satan's demise and defeat are already a certainty. The crafting of the gallows from which he will hang himself is the sum total of all of his rebellion and efforts.

You Can Choose

The Jewish Holocaust survivor and psychologist Viktor Frankl said, "Everything can be taken from a man or a woman but one thing: the last of the human freedoms—to choose one's attitude in any given set of circumstances, to choose one's own way."

I have been to Auschwitz, and I cannot begin to describe the horror I felt in the memory of the sheer evil that took place there. Dr. Frankl observed that those who survived had one thing in common. It was their willpower to not relinquish their ability to choose. No matter how much hatred and injustice they suffered, they refused to allow the Nazi soldiers to take away their right to choose how they would respond. Many times they chose forgiveness over resentment, anger, and hatred. Their souls received life-giving breaths of strength, drinking the sweet nectar of liberation in the midst of every kind of cruelty, hostility, and bondage experienced during their captivity.

My friend, you have been given the right to choose. You have a free will despite the teaching of some. Do not believe them. The loss of free will equates to the loss of power and therefore the abdication of responsibility! After all, if you have no free will, how could you be responsible for your actions and choices? Sadly, to many this abdication is a preference, but please understand your authority in life is directly correlated to the level of responsibility you take for your life. Those who assume no responsibility have given away all authority and have rendered themselves victims. God did not make you a victim; He created you to have dominion and rule over the earth and its beasts.

It cost God a great deal to give you this free will. Tragically, today many of us have yielded our free will to become slaves and victims living far below God's best for our lives.

How Can I Know the Will of God?

I beseech you therefore, brethren, by the mercies of God, that you present your bodies a living sacrifice, holy, acceptable to God, which is your reasonable service. And do not be conformed to this world, but be transformed by the renewing of your mind, that you may prove what is that good and acceptable and perfect will of God. (Rom. 12:1–2)

If everything that happens isn't God's will, then whose will is it? Great question. The answer is *man's will*. What I mean by that is man's will makes up the breach. We can only be brought into judgment one day because we have been given the will to choose as we please, be it right or wrong, good or bad. We have complete freedom to choose what we like without any interference from God. We will be judged according to our choices based upon God's laws of right and wrong and our knowledge of them.

Intercession: Mandatory or Optional?

Okay, I acknowledge that some of you are already feeling very uncomfortable and nervous at the thought that not everything is the will of God—like a giant rug is about to be pulled out from under you revealing instead that the ground you stand on is not sure and secure. Well, let me pose a question to you: If the will of God was automatic and always happened, why would Jesus, who has completed the work of God and is seated at the right hand of the Father, be in a place where He is always making intercession for us? If God's will was automatic, then no intercession would be necessary on behalf of the saints and especially by the Son of God, who said, "It is finished!" Look at Hebrews 7:25: "Therefore He is able also to save forever those who draw near to God through Him, since He always lives to make intercession for them" (NASB).

I believe that the Bible has a very strong theme that at the right-hand side of the throne of God Christ our Savior sits and it is there that He makes intercession for us. When the sheep are separated from the goats, Jesus tells us that condemnation resides on the left-hand side of the throne of God while salvation lies on the right-hand side. The Bible, my friend, makes it very clear that there is a battle going on in Middle-earth and you and I are engaged in it whether we want to admit it or participate in it or not. Without intercession, prayer, and engagement, the perfect will of God remains suspended in a perpetual state of challenge! Let me show you by taking you back—way back.

How Many Wills Are at Play in Our Universe?

I used to believe for the longest time that there were three wills at play in our universe. I thought they were the will of God, the will of man, and the will of the devil. Then one day as we were sitting down to have a family meal, our daughter, Zoe, then two years old, decided to sit in her big brother's place as he was delaying his arrival at the family table. She then proceeded to pick up his knife and promptly place it in her mouth. Shocked, I said, "Zoe, don't do that—it's dangerous! Give me the knife." To which she pulled away and replied defiantly, "No! Mine!"

It hit me like a ton of bricks. There are not three wills at play in our universe—there are some seven billion plus! It dawned on me that to remove himself from God's kingdom, all Adam had to do was take the fruit from the forbidden tree, because that statement was a statement of exclusion. Adam was saying, "Not Thy will, but my will be done!" Or, in Zoe language, "No! Mine!"

How do you know if you are in the kingdom? It's relatively easy—whose will do you live for? "Thy kingdom come, thy will be done in earth, as it is in heaven" (Matt. 6:10 KJV). The kingdom can only come through His will being done, or else how can His kingdom come? You can choose not to be part of the kingdom by simply deciding you do not like His will and therefore will not be abiding by it.

That's why when Jesus, the second Adam, comes onto the scene, we also find Him in a garden. Adam was in a garden called Eden (paradise), but Jesus was in a garden called Gethsemane, which literally means "oil press." It was in that very different garden, under incredible duress, that Jesus sweat drops of blood, fell on His face, and prayed, "Father, if there is any way this cup can pass by without me drinking it, please . . . nevertheless, not my will, but Thy will be done!" That statement saved the world! The first Adam chose to do his own will and ended up in bondage. The second Adam chose to do God's will and ended all bondage.

Free Will Means You Can Build Your Own Kingdom

In the book of Genesis we find an interesting story in chapter 11. It's the story of the Tower of Babel:

> Now the whole earth had one language and one speech. And it came to pass, as they journeyed from the east, that they found a plain in the land of Shinar, and they dwelt there. Then they said to one another, "Come, let us make bricks and bake them thoroughly." They had brick for stone, and they had asphalt for mortar. And they said, "Come, let us build ourselves a city, and a tower whose top is in the heavens; let us make a name for

ourselves, lest we be scattered abroad over the face of the whole earth." But the LORD came down to see the city and the tower which the sons of men had built. And the LORD said, "Indeed the people are one and they all have one language, and this is what they begin to do; now nothing that they propose to do will be withheld from them. Come, let Us go down and there confuse their language, that they may not understand one another's speech." So the LORD scattered them abroad from there over the face of all the earth, and they ceased building the city. Therefore its name is called Babel, because there the LORD confused the language of all the earth; and from there the LORD scattered them abroad over the face of all the earth. (vv. 1–9)

This is a fascinating story and one that beautifully highlights the conflict that resides on our planet and within each human heart. Always remember, our external world is simply a manifestation of our internal world. The world we have created around us is the result of choices we have made based upon values and priorities that lie within us (in our hearts).

God gave man a direct command to "be fruitful and multiply; fill the earth and subdue it" (Gen. 1:28). However, by Genesis 11, man had decided that he did not want to obey God's directive and decided instead to do something completely contrary to the will of God. Instead of scattering across the earth, they decided to gather in one place to build a tower that reached the heavens. This wasn't so they could get closer to God, but so that men would marvel at their accomplishments and magnificence. They wanted to make a name for themselves. They did not want to lift up the name of the Lord. Instead of doing God's will, they were doing their own will, and it was so contrary to God's will and command that God Himself had to come down and intervene by confusing their language. God said, "Indeed the people are one and they all have one language, and this is what they begin to do; now nothing that they propose to do will be withheld from them" (Gen. 11:6). In other words, they would have success outside of God's purpose!

Ouch! That means that just because something is successful does not mean that it's automatically God's will.

In Isaiah 14:12–14, we see how Lucifer decided that he wanted to build his own kingdom where he was the object of worship and where he was revered as God. He fell from heaven because he no longer desired to do God's will, just his own.

There are so many wills at play that God's will is almost shut out and banished into the background noise of a world bent on satiating its own lusts, wills, and desires.

When Jesus came to earth, He came to show us the Father. In other words, He came to show us what God was really like. The Israelites only partially saw who God was because so much of Him was hidden behind His laws. Because He is just, His righteous justice executed judgment upon transgressors time and time again, leading the Israelites to believe that it certainly is a fearful thing to fall into the "hands of an angry God," as Jonathan Edwards, the famous Great Awakening preacher, spoke in 1741.[1]

However, when Jesus came, He showed that even though He wrote the law to make us aware of sin and its consequences, His highest desire was not our destruction and damnation but rather our deliverance and salvation. These things are evident when we look at the Scriptures through the life of Christ, but they are hidden, or at least partially eclipsed, when we are only looking at the law. Jesus went about healing people, restoring life, bringing liberty, opening the eyes of the blind, teaching the love of the Father for a sinful world, and restoring hope and purpose into people's lives. Then in the most powerful display of love *ever* witnessed on planet Earth, He gave His life upon a Roman cross to redeem our souls. There has never been a demonstration of love that even compares to this in all of human history. Jesus in one fell swoop injects the antidote to the self-centeredness that has corrupted our universe with the most potent display of selfless sacrifice ever. That's why He deserves to be worshiped as God. Only God is that magnificent and perfect!

God's Perfect Will Is Not Primary but Secondary

If God's will were primary, then everyone would indeed be a praying Christian who daily woke up saying the words of Darth Vader, "What is thy bidding, my master?" There would be no rapes, murders, violence, thefts, drugs, and so on. But the Bible says that "all have sinned and fall short of the glory of God" (Rom. 3:23) and, "All we like sheep have gone astray; we have turned, every one, to his own way; and the LORD has laid on Him the iniquity of us all" (Isa. 53:6).

Does this mean that God is not able to protect me? He absolutely can, but because He gave man free will and will not violate man's ability to choose most of the time, we live in God's "permissible will." His perfect will comes to the earth through human beings who surrender themselves to doing His will with total devotion and selflessness. It's an act of your will that requires a daily surrender. Perhaps that's why His mercies are new every morning. I know that my heart constantly frets with wanting to please myself at the expense of the Lord. It is a disease we will live with until the end of all things when Jesus returns and delivers us completely!

Be encouraged, though, because even in the midst of a world that only dwells in God's permissible will with infrequent punctuations of His perfect will, God is so powerful and brilliant that He is able to make "all things work together for good to those who love God, to those who are the called according to His purpose" (Rom. 8:28). He can turn around pretty much anything to make it work for good when we love Him and trust Him with our hearts.

When we pray we create a conduit in the earth that allows heaven and God's perfect will to come into play and affect the earth. This is what Jesus meant when He said to His followers, "You are the salt of the earth . . . you are the light of the world" (Matt. 5:13, 14). Those characteristics were only ever ascribed to God before Jesus came. Jesus was not giving us an unwarranted promotion, but rather telling us that as believers we will bring salt and light to a world that without us would be violated and consumed by the darkness. This happens every time we pray, gather in worship, preach the Word, and proclaim the gospel of the kingdom!

TEN

The Lion King

Every kingdom divided against itself is brought to desolation, and every city or house divided against itself will not stand. If Satan casts out Satan, he is divided against himself. How then will his kingdom stand? And if I cast out demons by Beelzebub, by whom do your sons cast them out? Therefore they shall be your judges. But if I cast out demons by the Spirit of God, surely the kingdom of God has come upon you. Or how can one enter a strong man's house and plunder his goods, unless he first binds the strong man? And then he will plunder his house.
—MATTHEW 12:25-29

One of my favorite movies is *The Lion King*. Even though it's a kid's movie I love it and have taken my wife to see the Broadway musical version and we both sang along and enjoyed the costumes and the retelling of this awesome story! The movie and Broadway production highlight a kingdom in conflict and the power struggles that vie for ultimate authority within it. Its correlation to the biblical condition is striking. Whether this was intentional by the writer/director I am not sure. However, I do know that the character Scar, whom I believe is a type of Lucifer, ascends to the throne and thereby sentences the Pride Land to starvation and chaos—much like all that comes under the rule or governance of the devil.

With the kingdom in demise Scar is more than reluctant to admit fault and will not voluntarily relinquish the throne and the exalted position that comes with it.

Scar *must be* challenged by way of a confrontation with the rightful heir, Simba, who is the son of the benevolent king, Mufasa. Once Simba steps up and challenges Scar there is a clash and a battle between them, which sees Simba rise triumphant and Scar evicted from the throne and the kingdom.

This is a powerful portrait of what Jesus taught us in the verse opening this chapter about how prayer effectively works in the heavenly realm. Simba represents you and I as the sons of the most high and the rightful heirs to the throne of the kingdom. However, like Simba, we have to push through the devil's devices of shame, guilt, condemnation, and unholy alliances to confront him and dethrone him! It required more than courage. It required a reminder from his heavenly father of his true identity.

Mufasa speaking from the clouds in the heavens above him heralds, "Simba, you are my son, but you've forgotten who you are. Remember, remember who you are, you are my son . . . Remember!" At that Simba remembers, and courage rises, synergizing with this newfound knowledge, whereby he marches back to the Pride Land to restore law and order!

That is PUSH in movie form. You and I are "heirs with Christ"

(Rom. 8:17) and therefore rightful possessors of the authority of the kingdom. However, the devil has usurped the throne and everything under his rule becomes vacant, corrupt, and uninhabitable. Like Scar he will not relinquish the throne but must be displaced.

A Not-So-Heavenly Encounter

In 1991 I was a second-year Bible college student, and my sister-in-law graciously allowed me to stay in the three-bedroom seaside apartment that she and her husband owned in the city of Newcastle, Australia. I was to speak in a high school assembly one morning, and the apartment's close proximity to the school made it a perfect place to stay (being right across the road from the surf may also have had something to do with it!). The school was a state school that had not had a clergyman speak in a long time, although I considered myself anything but a clergyman.

I knew I was going to have my work cut out for me the next day, as speaking to hundreds of high school students is a difficult task most of the time. However, it's only made tougher by the introduction the headmaster usually brings. It tends to remove any coolness or affinity with the students I may have tried to smuggle into the school. I have seen confident speakers not recover from this deficit. I knew I would have to know my points, my jokes, my stories, and my facts or I would be eaten alive. Furthermore, I wasn't thinking of surviving but of thriving and smashing preconceived ideas about God and opening up these young hearts to the infinite love of an amazing Savior!

The school had been through a lot of turmoil in recent months. There were reports reaching the education department that teachers were indulging in illicit narcotics along with the students, and a spate of teen pregnancies had only added to the battles the school was facing within the community. It really was a school in deep trouble, quickly losing credibility with parents. I guess the principal must have thought, *What can it hurt to have a Bible college student speak in the assembly?*

I was on the third day of a three-day fast; being a zealous Bible college student I so wanted to be used of God and was not leaning upon my gift or ability. After I spent a good hour in pretty intense prayer for the school, I decided it was time to hit the hay and get a good night's sleep. I knew I would need to be at my best to make a difference in this school. What happened next was freaky!

I awoke with a fright as I felt someone or something on top of me. Hands gripped my throat as fear coursed through my body. I tried to distinguish who or what it was that was attacking me. It felt as though my very life force was being sucked out of my body. I cried out to God, "Lord, You are here in this room—You see what's going on. Help me!" At that the Lord simply said to me, *Pray in tongues!* I thought, *Pray in tongues? This thing's trying to kill me, and you're asking me to pray in languages I don't understand?* So instead I tried to rebuke the dark force by using the name that is above every other name, the name of Jesus!

Well, I could not get the words out, no matter how hard I tried. Then the Holy Spirit said to me again, *Pray in tongues.* As I began to pray in tongues, immediately the thing's grip began to loosen. I began to feel relief in my lungs, like the life force it was trying to suck out of me was being revived. Then all of a sudden I felt power pulsate through my body, and I yelled, "In the name of Jesus, get out of here!" *Bam!* Just like that, the demonic spirit left.

The atmosphere in the room immediately changed, becoming peaceful and light. So I did what a brave man of God would do next—I jumped up and turned on the light. (Well, maybe not so brave.) The Holy Spirit showed me that this spirit was the "strong man" over the school. I felt Him say, *You are invading his territory; you are walking into the arena of his dominion. But fear not, I have called you to take dominion over everything that creeps on the earth.*

For the next forty minutes or so I prayed with great fervency and authority against that demonic spirit and for the school. I found myself declaring that the demon was bound in the name of Jesus. I declared that it no longer had any power over the school, over the students, over the faculty, over their minds and lives, but was bound by a stronger man (Christ!). It was a revelation to me. I had never considered myself to be a stronger man, but in Christ we are more than conquerors. We are *in Christ* and He is *in us.* Therefore, "He who is in you is greater than he who is in the world" (1 John 4:4).

The next day, when I got up to preach, a hush fell over the students as they listened intently and laughed at most of my jokes. I preached out of my shoes—stuff was coming to me that was not in my notes. It was like I had been bitten by a radioactive spider or had a big red *S* on my chest. Then the time came to give an appeal to the 600-plus students seated, completely attentive to my address. No one was moving, and when I asked for people to raise their hands to respond to Christ two-thirds of the students and many of the faculty responded. It was such a powerful morning, one I would not soon forget, but I knew that it was due to the power of prayer.

Powerless prayer—the kind of prayer that is not PUSH prayer—is to pray without understanding and without knowledge of what Christ has done for us and who we are in the kingdom as "joint heirs with Christ" (Rom. 8:17). Too many unwittingly trade these biblical truths for "sincerity and piety." Not that these things are bad, but when it comes to ground-taking prayer, groveling unfortunately does not cut it. If God has elevated us to be seated "in Christ, at His right hand," how can we think that we curry favor and impress Him by groveling around in the dirt, confessing that we are nothing but worms? Did Jesus die for worthless worms? He gave His life for us, and therefore we must have some value, even if we don't see it. There is a saying in the real estate trade, that the *value* of a property is not determined so much by what the owner has put into it but rather what someone is willing to pay for it. There has been no higher price paid for you and me. Let's not insult God when we pray but rather approach God with gratitude for what He has done in Christ!

Permissible or Perfect?

Unless we pray until something happens, we will remain in the permissible will of God, where the will of man or the will of the devil remains the dominant influence. Let me explain this to you.

My youngest son earned forty dollars one month and begged

to go to Target immediately to spend his newfound small fortune. I wanted him to save it, and suggested as much. He, however, wanted to buy LEGOs. I even tried to sweeten the deal, telling him I would pay him interest if he saved it, but alas, his heart was set on the thought of spending his money on whatever he desired, and nothing would dissuade him. The euphoria of walking out with a tangible reward in exchange for a few menial tasks was written all over his face, and the repeated suggestions of saving it up were drowned out like background chatter in a discotheque. He was focused. Was it my perfect will and desire for his money to be spent this way? No, but it was no longer my money; it was his, and as immature as he was when it came to spending and saving, he had earned the money, so it was his jurisdiction as to how he was going to spend it.

Because it was his money, I had to allow him to spend the money as he saw fit, while I stood by thinking of much wiser choices. I knew a high value needed to be placed on delayed gratification, but my youngest could not yet see it as it was eclipsed by the benefit of immediate gain from spending his loot. It was not my perfect will—it was his will. However, as a loving father, I did permit it. Today he has lost many pieces of that LEGO and probably would have been better off saving the money and adding to it so that in the future he could buy himself a car or something awesome.

I believe that this is how the kingdom of God operates on the earth. God has given dominion to man, and yet He retains a desire and a perfect will for our lives. He allows us the freedom to choose, undergirding our choices with His perfect love and guidance, not limiting His rescuing us from ourselves to just once. God communicates His will to us by His written Word in the Bible. This is why it is so important to build a daily habit of reading it. But God leaves every final decision up to us; He does not force His will upon us. He merely guides, prompts, and suggests that His ways may not only be higher than our ways, but also far better!

Jesus acknowledges that Satan is indeed the "ruler of this world." So let me make the following statement: the permissible will of God *is* the default position of the earth!

Genesis 1 tells us that in the beginning God created the heavens and the earth, and the earth was without form. Void and darkness covered the face of the deep. Darkness is the default position of the universe. God had to speak His Word into the universe to bring forth light from the darkness, and it is the same today. The absence of God's Word in regions, countries, and even our lives leaves us grappling and stumbling in the darkness.

Your life, without the Word of God, will move toward darkness and chaos. Society, without the Word of God, moves toward darkness and chaos. Case in point, the former USSR, which threw God and His Word out of Eastern Europe. Their belief (made popular through the teachings of Marx, Lenin, and Nietzsche) was that man could govern better and create a utopia if only God and His pesky Bible were completely removed and the power vacuum filled by men with good intentions. The men would rule and make sure everybody had the same amount—nobody had more and nobody had less. Obviously they would be excluded, as they deserved to have more. They deserved the best food, wine, lodging, and wealth. They brought about misery, destruction, poverty, and suffering unrivaled in their time. But at least they only had to murder twenty-six million of their people to bring about that wonderful, atheistic utopian society![1]

Is God a Killer of Sparrows?

When Jesus said in Matthew 10:29, "Are not two sparrows sold for a copper coin? And not one of them falls to the ground apart from your Father's will," He was not saying that God spends His days killing sparrows. He was saying that God is in control and that He is aware of the death of the sparrow and has permitted it. However, when Jesus taught us to pray, He said, "Thy kingdom come, Thy will be done on earth as it is in heaven" (Matt. 6:10 KJV). For God's kingdom to come, people have to choose His will over their own. His kingdom is unlike any earthly kingdom that usually takes ground and establishes its rule by force and servitude. God is not like this. We have to choose to make Him our Lord and God for His kingdom to come into our lives.

Jesus prayed that God's will be done on earth "as it is in heaven," meaning that on earth His will is *not* done as it is in heaven. Otherwise, why say it? Am I saying that God's will is not being done on earth as it is in heaven? No, Jesus is saying it! Jesus is not using hyperbole or embellishing the facts—He is telling us the truth. *But how come Jesus said that "a sparrow doesn't fall to the ground apart from my Father's will"?* Because Jesus is telling us the earth lives in the *permissible* will of God, not in His perfect will. Our job is to bring His perfect will to earth, but to do so we have to PUSH!

Bartimaeus was born blind; was that God's perfect will? No, we see God's perfect will in his encounter with Jesus. Jesus said to him, "Go your way; your faith has made you well," upon which he immediately received his sight (Mark 10:52). The perfect will of God requires faith. Faith is not a passive, private believing, but a practiced, applied, forceful engagement in prayer and word. God spoke into the darkness, "Let there be light." He didn't think it, wish it, hope it, or dream it—He *spoke* it into being! The permissible will of God is the natural state of our fallen world. We are called to override this with the perfect will of God. This can only happen through prayer, intercession, spiritual warfare, faith, and most powerfully, the speaking of truth (God's Word).

Heaven Is the Measure of the Will of God

In the gospel of Luke, chapter 13, a woman had a spirit of infirmity for eighteen years. Was that God's perfect will for her life? Of course not! If that person were in heaven right now, what would she be experiencing? Would Satan be oppressing her? Will there be blind people walking around in heaven with guide dogs leading them? Will there be paralyzed or disabled people in wheelchairs? Will there be death, pain, and suffering in heaven? Will there be divorce, disease, and infirmity in heaven? Will there be poverty and starvation in heaven? The answer to all of these is no!

This is how we see and understand God's perfect will. Jesus said, "Thy will be done on earth *as it is in heaven*." When Jesus met the woman with the spirit of infirmity, He laid His hands upon her back, saying to her, "Woman, you are loosed from your infirmity," upon which she immediately straightened up (v. 12). What happened? The perfect will collided with the permissible will, and the perfect will overcame the permissible will.

We have been misinformed. We have been taught that pain, suffering, misery, sickness, and disease are all part of God's perfect will and are tools that the Almighty implements as teaching aids to instruct our lives. How can you actively resist something that you have been told is actually from God and should therefore be embraced with thanksgiving, because God is good? It's interesting that Jesus was called "rabbi," which means "teacher," yet He went about *healing* people of all kinds of sickness and disease, casting out demon spirits, and teaching in the synagogues about the king- dom of God! Not once did He give someone a sickness or disease as He taught. He never went up to a person while He was teaching and said to him or her, "Here is some sickness, a little terminal ill- ness for ya. You're welcome! (wink) It's just God's way of teaching you about the preciousness of life." Yet today much teaching in the church would have you believe that this is exactly what God does.

A widow in Nain lost her only son and as a result would lose all means of financial support and provision. As she was leaving the city, her sorrow was evident and her future bleak. She was trying to come to grips with the permissible will of God. However, when her party encountered Jesus' party coming into the gate of the city, there was a clash of two sons. One son was dead and represented the permissible will of God, and the other Son was Jesus Christ, who is the carrier of the perfect will of God! Jesus, upon seeing the woman in the depths of grief, put out His hand and stopped the funeral party in its tracks. He then said, "Young man, I say to you, arise" (Luke 7:14). The young man arose and was restored to life.

This again is a potent picture of the perfect will of God triumphing over the permissible.

How Does the Will of God Come to Pass?

This is how God establishes His perfect will on the earth over His permissible will: He sends His Word into the earth. His Word is rejected and resisted by those forces in the earth that want to rule independently of Him because He threatens their autonomy and rule. Accepting His Word means accepting His sovereignty and lordship. However, His Word is both accepted and received by those who are for His kingdom and accept Him as their Lord and sovereign. They now become the recipients of His Word and have the task of establishing His Word on the earth. To do this they must push through the resistant forces in the world to plant the Word into the soil of the earth and bear kingdom of heaven fruit. This is done through the exercising of prayer, obedience, and the declaration by faith of the Word of God. The acceptance of the Word results in His kingdom and perfect will coming to pass. That's why the preaching of the Word is so important. Without the Word the will of God cannot come to pass.

Seed Kingdom

The kingdom of God resides in His Word. His Word is the seed that produces His kingdom. In a seed resides the DNA for what the future is to be. When God's Word is sent, spoken, received, and planted into the hearts of believers, it produces the kingdom of God on earth. His Word is not only the seed of the kingdom of God, but in His Word also resides His perfect will. In the absence of His Word being spoken, His permissible will prevails.

In His permissible will, He has allowed a season where Satan will reign. In His permissible will, there is a season where "Jerusalem will be trampled under foot by the Gentiles" (Luke 21:24 NASB). In His permissible will, there will be wars and rumors of wars, famines, violence, murder, persecution, and oppression in its varying forms. But when His Word comes and it is received, it changes nations and kingdoms because it changes hearts. Other religions may change behavior, but only the Word of God can change the state of the human heart. That's why every other religion makes you change the outside—your dress, hair, etc.—to conform. Only Christianity contains the power to transform, because it alone has the Word of God.

Satan *hates* the Word of God not only because it contains the DNA of the kingdom of God in which he no longer resides, but also because within it resides God's perfect will, which triumphantly overcomes His permissible will (where Satan currently resides). The more the Word advances, the more Satan's dominion decreases. The Bible says that Satan has been cast down to the earth: "Therefore rejoice, O heavens, and you who dwell in them! Woe to the inhabitants of the earth and the sea! For the devil has come down to you, having great wrath, because he knows that he has a short time" (Rev. 12:12). Satan knows that the sand in the hourglass is diminishing by the moment; however, the end will not come until this gospel of the kingdom is preached to the whole world (Matt. 24:14). So you need to understand that for Satan, opposing the gospel is not a matter of preference but one of life and death. With everything in him he opposes the preaching of the Word of God so that he can extend his rule and delay the inevitable.

So, to summarize, the Word of God is the seed that produces the kingdom of God. Within the Word of God resides the DNA of not only the kingdom of God but also His perfect will. When spoken, received, and planted, the Word of God will always produce kingdom results and bring about God's perfect will. Look at Jesus' life: wherever He went, He spoke and people were healed, delivered, and even raised from the dead. God's will is life, health, abundance, peace, and freedom: "The thief does not come except to steal, and to kill, and to destroy. I have come that they may have life, and that they may have it more abundantly" (John 10:10). There is nothing more powerful in the universe than the Word of God.

Psalm 119:89 says: "Forever, O Lord, Your word is settled in heaven." The word *settled* is a peculiar word in Hebrew and literally means "established" or "secured," as in a group of watchmen establishing ground and setting up a secure perimeter around it. This is what the Word does when spoken into your circumstances. It has prevailing power to trump whatever has been permitted in order to establish what is perfect. It is as powerful today as it was aeons ago when God first spoke, "Let there be light!" Because His Word is eternal, it never becomes outdated; the only thing that changes over the centuries are the mouths that carry the Word of God. Today, let your mouth become the contemporary instrument that speaks and declares the eternal Word of God into this present time and moment.

God Is an Invitation-Only God

Perhaps the devil's cleverest ploy so far has been to make us believe that prayer is both pointless and powerless—that God will do whatever He wants to do anyway because He is sovereign! The Bible teaches the exact opposite of this. When we pray, things happen. God said, "If my people who are called by My name will humble themselves, and pray and seek My face, and turn from their wicked ways, then I will hear from heaven, and will forgive their sin and heal their land" (2 Chron. 7:14).

A God *who suffered*

> *For God to create all He had to do was speak,*
> *but for God to redeem He had to suffer.*
> —AUTHOR UNKNOWN

You can hear the lament of the heart of God in Ezekiel 22:30: "So I sought for a man among them who would make a wall, and stand in the gap before Me on behalf of the land, that I should not destroy it; but I found no one." His will was not for the city to be destroyed, so He searched high and low for just one person who would intercede, who would build a wall, who would *cry out* for the city, but He found no one, and sadly the city ended up being destroyed.

The saddest believers I have ever met are the "judgment-happy" ones, who seem to revel in cities being destroyed because of the judgment of God upon the sin of that city. We see them picket our fallen soldiers' funerals, condemning them for their bravery and sacrifice. Their signs and their chants tell us that they are purveyors of hate not love. They completely miss the heart of God. He isn't looking for someone to stand there and throw stones at fallen mankind. He is looking for someone to build a wall, to stand in the gap and cry out on behalf of the city, believing for its salvation instead of its destruction.

We see a God who is not unaccustomed to pain. In Genesis chapter 6 His heart is broken because the thoughts and intents of man's heart are only evil continually. He deeply regrets making man, overwhelmed by the pain of the disappointment He feels for His creation in moral mutiny. Our God who responds to prayer waits with longing for us to turn from our sins, to get sick and tired of being sick and tired, and cry out for a change, a revolution, a resolution, for Him.

Abraham cried out to God when God revealed His plan to destroy Sodom and Gomorrah. Abraham's intercession saved the lives of Lot and his daughters. Likewise, when God wanted to wipe out the entire Israelite nation and make a new nation out of Moses, it was Moses who interceded again and again on behalf of the people so that today the nation of Israel is the nation that exists.

Necessity Is the Mother of All Invention

You may have heard this before, but you must also understand that what this is saying is that comfort is the enemy of progress. In other words, when we are comfortable we are not as motivated to invent ways to become more comfortable or to make life more convenient. Sadly it is also so when it comes to prayer. Why is it that the most fervent times of prayer in our lives are at the moments of crisis and desperation? This is why I love prayer as a regular practice. I find that when I pray, I access the heart of the Father through the Holy Spirit, and all of a sudden I am overwhelmed with the need to pray for many specific things. My prayer life becomes pregnant with need, hope, and a longing to see God move.

Too many people believe sickness, disease, and calamity are sent from God to teach us something. The Bible does indeed say that "all things work together for good to those who love God, to those who are the called according to His purpose" (Rom. 8:28), but that is far different from saying that God caused it to begin with. Yes, He will definitely use it, turn it around, and bring something positive out of it, but to say He caused it is misguided.

The World Is a Sin Haven, Not a Safe Haven

The Bible teaches that sin must run its course, and that God has not only allowed this to happen but also uses it to weed out those who want Him versus those who want to live for their own devices and pleasures. When Jesus taught the disciples to pray saying, "Thy kingdom come, Thy will be done on earth as it is in heaven," He was saying that the will of God is not the paramount and default position of the earth. He was telling us it could *only* come and be established through prayer.

Prayer is the engagement of the will of man to surrender to the will of God.

When Jesus preached His first sermon on the Mount of Olives, He proclaimed, "You are the salt and the light of the world." Interesting words to what I would have called "immature" believers. After all, that was His first sermon. I would have probably been tempted to interrupt Jesus and say, "Lord, I love Your heart, but why don't we wait until they show their true colors, whether they are flaky or committed, before we start telling them that they are such significant things as salt and light!" Jesus was not declaring what we could be; He was declaring what we *are*.

Salt is used in preservation. Obviously, in Jesus' time there was no refrigeration, so meat was salted to allow it to keep long enough for you to plan a banquet or meal without the guests dying of food poisoning. Light, we know, helps people to see where they are going. So "salt and light" is Jesus saying that without you, the world stumbles in darkness and will rot so much quicker. Without the presence of the church—God's elect—the world would quickly degenerate into anarchy and chaos. It's the believers who have held the torch and fought for human life, stood against abortion, brought about emancipation from slavery, and elevated women to an equal status with men.

When I say the world is a sin haven I am not advocating joining in with it, but rather presenting the mandate we have of overthrowing this system. It is this way because Scar is ruling and not the Lion King. However, when we pray we depose the prince of darkness and allow life, light, righteousness, and peace to flourish once again in those regions. It's time for the "Lion Kings" of the earth to rise, push back the powers of darkness by proclaiming the Word of God into the atmosphere over our homes, communities, and cities, and see Jesus Christ the King of kings glorified!

> Then the seventh angel sounded: And there were loud voices in heaven, saying, "The kingdoms of this world have become the kingdoms of our Lord and of His Christ, and He shall reign forever and ever!" (Rev. 11:15)

It's time the Lion Kings found their roar!

ELEVEN

Ocean's Eleven

*Every great movement of God can
be traced to a kneeling figure.*
—D. L. MOODY

In the movie *Ocean's Eleven*, Danny Ocean is played by actor George Clooney, who upon being released from a New Jersey prison already has his next big heist planned out. He is going to knock over three of the biggest casinos in Las Vegas and walk away with a cool $150 million dollars. Danny Ocean assembles a crack team of experts and the heist gets underway.

The Bible tells us in the book of Ephesians that when Jesus ascended on high He led captivity and gave gifts to men, some apostles, some prophets, some evangelists, and some pastors and teachers (4:11). In other words, Jesus, like Danny Ocean, assembles a "crack team" to plunder the kingdom of darkness.

This happens in every generation: men and women are equipped and empowered to pull off one great heist from the kingdom of darkness after another, bringing souls out of bondage and into glorious freedom.

Unlimited Treasury

As I was walking out of the office one day, I glanced over at the reception booth. There it was, staring at me, taunting me. It was an ad for the Faith Leadership Conference in Seattle, Washington, and I so wanted to go. It had all the heroes of the faith speaking at it and was heralded as the conference of conferences. Problem was, we had no money. Zilch, zip, none, nada! I could not afford to go. We were living half a world away in Auckland, New Zealand, quite an expensive place to live in the nineties. Our church was small so funds were always tight, and my senior pastor told me it would cost me about $2,500 if I wanted to go. This equated to a month and a half of our salary. My wife was pregnant at the time with our first child, so there was no room for any extras in our very tight budget. Back then we had no savings to speak of as we lived hand to mouth and month to month. I looked up at the poster one more time and muttered, "God, I'd really like to go to that!" (I felt a little cheeky, like when it's a hot day and you're at the gas station with your dad and you say, "Wow, I'd really like an ice cream!") To my surprise, God spoke to me and said, *If you have the faith, I have the cash!*

God would use this situation to show me that He has unlimited resources, and that the only limitation in my life would be my faith, not His. I looked up to heaven and said, "I accept the challenge!" For the next six weeks, I prayed for an hour each night, speaking and declaring that money was coming in, that plane tickets were purchased, that hotel rooms were booked, and that I was attending the conference. Well, in those six weeks, money came in from everywhere. It was crazy! I would be approached in church and someone would say, "Pastor, God told me to give you this!" and then he or she would hand me a wad of cash! I went to the mailbox and there was an envelope from the tax department with a refund I was not expecting. Money just seemed to find me.

It was like when Peter asked Jesus about paying the temple tax and Jesus said something along the lines of, "Yeah, good idea. Go down to the sea, cast in a hook, and the first fish you pull out, open up its mouth and pull out the money in there. Pay yours and my temple tax, and tell 'em to keep the change!"

> Nevertheless, lest we offend them, go to the sea, cast in a hook, and take the fish that comes up first. And when you have opened its mouth, you will find a piece of money; take that and give it to them for Me and you. (Matt. 17:27)

God has unlimited resources, because God alone can create something from nothing.

I discovered that day that in my life my problem would never be a resource problem so much as it would be a prayer or a faith problem (actually a lack of prayer and a lack of faith to be precise). Some of us have been brought up in church to feel guilty if we ask God for anything, as He has already given us Jesus and that should be enough. But this is not consistent with Scripture.

> He who did not spare His own Son, but delivered Him up for us all, how shall He not with Him also freely give us all things? (Rom. 8:32)

In other words, if God was willing to give His only begotten Son, He will not withhold any good thing from you, otherwise it would make those things of more value than Jesus. Nothing is. So we must come to understand that faith asks, or put another way, faith has an "ask" attached to it.

Get Your ASK into Gear

Jesus said, "Whatever things you ask when you pray, believe that you receive them, and you will have them" (Mark 11:24). Clearly Jesus invites us to exercise our faith by asking in prayer. How can you grow your faith if you never ask God for something and then believe Him for it? James, the brother of Jesus, echoed that when he challenged us with, "You do not have because you do not ask" (James 4:2). What are you asking God for? What are you presently believing God for? Faith is not wishing, and wishing is not praying. Praying involves asking, and asking involves believing. Believing involves praying it through in faith until you hold in your hands what you have held with your heart.

Pretty soon tickets were booked, and I was flying to the United States to attend the conference. God, through prayer, had brought me a whopping $2,800, giving me about $300 spending money, which I naively thought would last me for the ten days. Upon arriving in the US of A, I realized I would not make it and went into prayer again asking God for wisdom and provision. Once again I felt the Lord say to me that He would graciously provide for me so that

I would not miss a meal the entire trip. This would be a powerful time in my life where God was teaching me firsthand that He has no lack and there is no lack for those who trust in Him (Ps. 34:10)!

Upon reaching the last three days of the trip, unfortunately the money had run out. I had lunch and dinner covered but no breakfast. *Was God asking me to fast?* I wondered. On the morning of our checkout and return home, I asked the Lord, *What happened? If you wanted me to fast why didn't you just say so?* God said to me, *I did provide for you!* I was just about to argue the point with the Almighty when I looked toward the door and noticed something strange. Each day the cleaner would leave the "Do not disturb" door hangers on the bench beside the door and replace it with a fresh one. *How odd,* I thought.

I walked over and picked one up to discover that upon each door hanger was written "One full continental breakfast," with the date for each day of my stay there. All I had to do was bring it with me to the restaurant in the hotel and I would enjoy a wonderful breakfast! God had provided—I just didn't see it!

God will keep His promises. His Word is sure, and His promises are true. PUSH is praying from "ask" *to* "receive." Don't be afraid to ask. Your faith cannot grow unless you ask. Once you ask, you then need to believe. That is where the battle is won and lost. Since that conference trip I have realized that upon asking I need to exercise my faith and believe that God is able to provide, no matter what I see, feel, or even experience. God is not limited, but His provision can be limited in our lives by what we can or cannot believe Him for.

Limiting the Unlimited

Is it possible for us to limit a limitless God?

It seems almost preposterous to even consider that the Almighty could in any way be adversely affected by us mere mortals. Some of us might believe this to be akin to admitting that the Almighty has a weakness and therefore is not the Almighty! If He can be limited perhaps He is just mighty at best? Some resolve this by believing that because God is sovereign He could never be limited by anyone or anything!

In Psalm 78:40–42 we read, "How often they provoked Him in the wilderness, and grieved Him in the desert! Yes, again and again they tempted God, and *limited* the Holy One of Israel. They did not remember His power: the day when He redeemed them from the enemy" (emphasis mine). God charged the children of Israel with *limiting* Him in their lives. The Almighty was limited in bringing His power and perfect will into their lives because of their unbelief, complaining, and faithlessness. I don't know about you, but I do *not* want to limit God in my life. I want the fullness of His presence, power, and will to be operating at all times. If I were to buy a car with a V8 engine in it, I would not want to be running on only three or four cylinders. Yet so many Christians live unaware that they are indeed limiting God in their lives.

From Barren to Breakthrough

The Bible says that Abraham "believed in the LORD, and He accounted it to him for righteousness" (Gen. 15:6). Sarah had no baby, and like her hubby, Abraham, she was also well advanced in years and beyond childbearing age. Yet the Bible says that Abraham believed God and Sarah became pregnant! Don't ever think your faith is private and does not affect others. Abraham's faith changed the state of Sarah's womb. Now unlike some of the gimmicks out there, this does not work like *The Secret*, where you simply ask the universe for whatever you want and the universe will supply it as long as you believe it. Abraham received a word from God when He was sixty and then a reminder when he was ninety that God was going to give him a son, an heir from his own loins and from Sarah's womb. This word from the Lord is what Abraham stood on and fought in faith to see come to pass. We cannot just manufacture what we want; we must get a word from God and stand upon that in faith, believing that over our circumstances.

God loves faith. He has given us all a measure of faith. The exercising of the faith that God has given us can increase this faith. Faith pleases God. Faith moves God. Faith draws the power of God into your life. You can believe God. You have the ability to exercise faith. You can begin to change the confession of your mouth and instead of speaking doubt, unbelief, and negativity, you can speak faith, hope, and love.

The Woman Who Stole a Healing

I love the story in Luke 8 about the woman with the issue of blood. Talk about *Ocean's Eleven* and a heist. She had been hemorrhaging for twelve years. Her condition sapped her of energy, dignity, and vitality, leaving her in an anemic state, and it had also left her penniless. She was unable to enter the temple to worship because of Jewish law. She had suffered much at the hands of the physicians and did not get better but worse. When she heard about Jesus, she came behind Him in the crowd to touch the edge of His garment. It all sounds innocent enough, except that Jesus was focused on healing Jairus's daughter and was not expecting what happened next.

On His way to Jairus's house, the Bible records, the crowds were "thronging him" on every side. But then Jesus stopped abruptly, turned, and asked, "Who touched Me?" The disciples thought Jesus couldn't be serious, the truth was everyone within six feet was pawing at Him, trying to touch Him. Jesus said, "Somebody touched Me, for I perceived power going out from Me" (Luke 8:46). When the woman, knowing she could not hide it from the Lord, came and knelt down and told what had happened, He said to her, "Your faith has made you well" (v. 48).

Jesus had no *intent* to heal her, but just because He wasn't *intending* to heal her doesn't mean He wasn't *willing*. It seems unbelief shuts down the power of God and faith releases the power of God. This story shows us that the power of God flows toward those with faith. Faith comes from hearing, and hearing by the Word of God.

"For she said to herself, 'If only I may touch His garment, I shall be made well'" (Matt. 9:21). Hearing about Jesus and the miracles He was performing made her believe that He was her answer. She then began to confess that all she needed to do was touch His garment and she would be made whole. That anemic woman *pushed* through the crowd, touched Him from behind, and drew power out of Him into her body, putting an immediate stop to her hemorrhaging. She walked into heaven's vault and walked out with her healing. Danny Ocean would have been proud. Heck, he may even have hired her.

Prayer Develops Overcomers!

Prayer is the key to accessing the will of God! Even Jesus, who was also fully God, spent much of His time in prayer. Why? Because being fully human, He could also have gone the way of His flesh, so we find in the Scriptures that He was in constant prayer. In Gethsemane, He cried out three times for God to take the cup away so that He didn't have to drink it. His humanity wrestled with the perfect will of God for His life. Thank God He chose to do what His Father wanted, not what His flesh and humanity wanted, or we would have been completely lost. It's amazing to think about the risk that God took with His "rescue" mission. It could have all been lost in that one moment.

Scripture teaches us that it is our faith in God that overcomes the world—His promises and His perpetual faithfulness toward us (1 John 5:4). Faith comes from the knowledge that God is always true to His Word! Unlike man, who promises and does not always come through, God *always* delivers that which He has promised. Prayer, the Word, and good teaching in church are the building blocks of our faith. Be in prayer. Be in the Word. Be in a Bible-teaching church.

Boldness Because of Grace

"For we do not have a High Priest who cannot sympathize with our weaknesses, but was in all points tempted as we are, yet without sin. Let us therefore come boldly to the throne of grace, that we may obtain mercy and find grace to help in time of need" (Heb. 4:15–16). Wow, God's throne is now called the throne of grace. It used to be solely known as the place of judgment. What happened? Well, if we study the picture of the tabernacle in the Old Testament, we discover some incredibly powerful truths that unveil the will of God for mankind.

We know that all have sinned and fall short of the glory of God (Rom. 3:23). We also know that in our sinful state we are unable to approach the throne of God because we would enter into His direct presence and walk directly into judgment. That would end our lives right there.

In Exodus 33, Moses asked the Lord to show him His glory. God knew Moses had no idea what he was asking, so He accommodated his request. But God said to Moses:

> I will make all My goodness pass before you, and I will proclaim the name of the LORD before you. I will be gracious to whom I will be gracious, and I will have compassion on whom I will have compassion. . . . You cannot see My face; for no man shall see Me, and live. . . . Here is a place by Me, and you shall stand on the rock. So it shall be, while My glory passes by, that I will put you in the cleft of the rock, and will cover you with My hand while I pass by. Then I will take

away My hand, and you shall see My back; but My face shall not be seen. (vv. 19–23)

God said that He would cover Moses with His hand to protect him from His presence while He passed by. We cannot stand in God's glory unless we stand upon the rock and are covered by His hand.

Now I hope you are beginning to see that Jesus is the rock upon which we stand, and it was God's own hand that bought us salvation so that we have a covering to stand in His glory. People will attempt to pervert the character of God as one who is a mighty punisher, whose only intention is to smite people for their sins and indiscretions. All the way through the Bible we find that God is the one who covers our sins, shame, and nakedness.

Now back to the throne of grace. The Old Testament tabernacle was made up of three main parts, just like God is three in one and we are three in one (body, soul, and spirit). There was the outer court, then the Holy Place, and then the Holy of Holies. The Holy of Holies was separated by a large, thick veil. In the center of the Holy of Holies was the ark of the covenant, which was a wooden box made of acacia wood and overlaid with gold, representing Christ's humanity as well as His divinity. On the top of the ark was the mercy seat, a place where the priest would come once a year with the blood of a perfect lamb sacrifice and offer it for the propitiation of the sins of Israel. On either side of the mercy seat were the cherubim, two angels who faced one another and covered the mercy seat. Above the mercy seat was the glory of God.

Inside the ark of the covenant there were three sacred items:

the budding rod of Aaron, the pot of manna, and the two tablets of stone containing the Ten Commandments. The reason the ark was under the mercy seat and contained those items was because Jesus Christ is the completion of the Old Testament type. He is the "rod that has budded," or better yet, the chosen One of God; He is "the bread of heaven" that we eat of to receive eternal life; and He is the fulfillment of the law and commandments of God. Then, to display His incredible supremacy, He is also the perfect Lamb sacrificed on the altar whose blood covers the mercy seat and converts it into the throne of grace for all who believe in Him!

You can now "come boldly" (Heb. 4:16) to that throne room, walk right into His presence, ask for what you need, and receive forgiveness, grace, and whatever you require. But you must learn to push beyond your own mind, the part of the brain that remembers how unworthy you are, which prevents you from entering into all that God has for you. Jesus said, "You shall know the truth, and the truth shall make you free" (John 8:32). It's only the truth you know that can set you free; what is unknown lies dormant in your life. That's why so many believers constantly struggle with never feeling good enough for God or feeling like they are constantly letting God down. The focus is wrong because the theology is flawed. We come with our failures and sins to the throne of grace *knowing* Christ has completely fulfilled the demands of the law and by His death brought us life, as undeserving as we are. This makes me want to fall down in worship, and it actually empowers me to conquer my sins. But you have to *PUSH*, compelled by the truth.

PUSH = Believing

An entire generation was kept out of the promised land for forty years, even though experts say that it was nothing more than an eleven-day journey to get there from the wilderness. Now I can understand, with children and maybe some elderly folks not moving as quickly and needing frequent stops for rest, that maybe that trip could blow out to forty days. But forty *years*? Come on! Why so long? The answer to that question is perhaps not initially a positive one, and that may prevent most folks from wanting to discover it. The Scripture says that the children of Israel wandered in the wilderness for forty years because of *unbelief*! In other words, the Israelites not crossing the Jordan and possessing the promised land had nothing to do with geography. It also had nothing to do with resources, opportunity, weather, experience, or anything else we human beings like to blame for our lack of good fortune.

Some may say, "Well, then it must have been God's will for them to wander and die in the wilderness because that's what happened!" Yes, that was what happened, but remember God's permissible will always happens—God's perfect will requires some push on our behalf. It was God's perfect will for the entire nation of Israel to enter into the promised land. However, they failed to enter because of their unbelieving hearts. The land was right there in front of them for forty years. Physically they could have crossed over at any time, but they didn't because the issue was not physical but spiritual! It was their unbelief.

The Power of God Flows in Accordance with Our Beliefs

According to your faith let it be to you. (Matt. 9:29)

PUSH is believing the Word of God over the circumstances, the negative reports, and even the feelings of hopelessness, fear, and despondency that we may have. How do we push through? Simple—we meditate upon the Word of God! Look at this story from 2 Kings 7:1–2:

> Then Elisha said, "Hear the word of the LORD. Thus says the LORD: 'Tomorrow about this time a seah of fine flour shall be sold for a shekel, and two seahs of barley for a shekel, at the gate of Samaria.'" So an officer on whose hand the king leaned answered the man of God and said, "Look, if the LORD would make windows in heaven, could this thing be?" And [Elisha] said, "In fact, you shall see it with your eyes, but you shall not eat of it."

The context of this story is that the king of Syria besieged Samaria. The people of Samaria resorted to desperate measures, even cannibalism, eating their own children. Elisha brought the Word of the Lord at the desperate summoning of the king who had not looked to the Lord for help until things had become so desperate. Elisha issued the word from God, and the officer heard it but responded unbelievingly. The next day, God did a miracle through four lepers who stumbled across an abandoned Syrian army camp laden with food and all kinds of treasures. The officer saw the miracle, but before he was able to partake in it, he was trampled by the stampeding horde of starving Samaritans. He wasn't punished *for* his unbelief (in case you're thinking that God is a punitive God); he was punished *by* his unbelief. Our unbelief restricts the power of God in our lives. We will see God's power manifest in our lives in direct accordance to our believing.

Push into the promises of God and walk in the pursuit of discovering the goodness and faithfulness of the God who has made these promises. He is good, always faithful, and He is for you.

Effective or Infected?

And when they had come to the multitude, a man came to Him, kneeling down to Him and saying, "Lord, have mercy on my son, for he is an epileptic and suffers severely; for he often falls into the fire and often into the water. So I brought him to Your disciples, but they could not cure him." Then Jesus answered and said, "O faithless and perverse generation, how long shall I be with you? How long shall I bear with you? Bring him here to Me." And Jesus rebuked the demon, and it came out of him; and the child was cured from that very hour. Then the disciples came to Jesus privately and said, "Why could we not cast it out?" So Jesus said to them, "Because of your unbelief; for assuredly, I say to you, if you have faith as a mustard seed, you will say to this mountain, 'Move from here to there,' and it will move; and nothing will be impossible for you. However, this kind does not go out except by prayer and fasting." (Matt. 17:14–21)

This is a powerful story of contrast with some powerful lessons in it for us. Jesus had just been transfigured on the mountaintop with Peter, James, and John. His clothes began to glow, and the disciples were completely terrified. When He returned from the Mount of Transfiguration, He rejoined the other nine disciples who did not go with Him up onto the mountain to seek God, but were instead in the village and in the marketplace. Jesus found them struggling to cast a demon out of a young boy. The father, desperate for relief for his son, brought the young lad to the disciples, but they could not cast out the demon. What a sad day and what a sad verse. Why is it sad? Because just seven chapters earlier, Jesus gave His disciples power over unclean spirits, to cast out demons, and to heal the sick. Just seven chapters later, we find them failing and seemingly powerless.

When the disciples asked Jesus, "Why could we not cast it out?" Jesus did not respond, "Because I am God and you are just mere flesh, walking dust, only human. You don't have the power for this kind of stuff—this is big boy's stuff!" No, Jesus said, "Because of your unbelief"! He also spoke of what an unbelieving and perverse generation they were living in. Not much has changed. The culture was toxic to faith in God. The disciples had become infected by this culture and were therefore no longer effective. You must understand, when God says, "Be holy as I am holy," the word *holy* means "to be separate or totally unique." God wants us to be separate so that we do not become infected with unbelief because of the toxicity of the faithlessness and perversion in our society all around us. It is a toxic culture—toxic to miracle-working faith and power!

Unbelief Is a Power Thief

In the same story, Jesus asked the father how long this had been happening to the lad. The father answered, "Since he was a child." The father continues "Lord, if you can do anything, please help us!" Jesus' response was immediate and direct. "If *you* can believe, all things are possible for him who believes." At that the man replied to Jesus, "Lord I believe; help my unbelief!" (Mark 9:22–25).

Unbelief played an obvious part in the young lad's ongoing suffering and in the delay of his deliverance. The secularization of the world in which we live has contaminated our culture to have little faith in God. We are like the boiling frogs who are happy to hop into the pot while the water is cool, but are completely unaware of the water being heated because it has been so slow and gradual around them that they have adjusted to it and accepted it as normal. The only answer is to push to "reset" a new normal by meditating on the Word of God daily!

The Word of God feeds your faith, which in turn fuels belief. This releases God's power and promises to flow into your life.

Not What but How

Many years ago, I heard the story of a US-based shoe company sending their young sales director to the African continent in the hopes of expanding their market share. After eighteen months of travel and study, the young director wrote a letter back to the head office saying, "Please send me a return fare; it's useless, no one in Africa wears shoes!" They did so and promptly brought the young man home. Not long after that, management changed at the company and the new leadership decided to once again try and reach into the continent of Africa. Another young sales director was dispatched, and this time after twelve months of extensive travel and study, the young man sent a telegram back to the head office. It read, "Please send all the shoes you can. No one in Africa wears shoes!"

Both men saw the same issues. But it wasn't *what* they saw—it was *how* they saw that made the difference in this story. Let God open your eyes to a "whole new world, a new fantastic point of view . . ." Sorry, I started singing there.

When the Holy Spirit is invited to quicken the Word of God into our hearts, it opens the eyes of our understanding. We have to live in the world, but we can choose to shape the world around us rather than be shaped by it! Below is a list of symptoms that I have pulled from the wilderness wanderings of the Israelites. If you see any of these in your life, then it is a good sign you need to spend more time exposed to the Word and less time exposed to the world.

Symptoms of an unbelieving heart

- Complaining (Num. 11:1)
- Gossip
- Negativity
- Slandering those in authority rather than honoring them
- Rebellion
- Lust
- Lying

- Fear
- Hopelessness
- Diminished vision
- Laying blame
- Wanting to go back to how it used to be, even though you hated it back then and were complaining then too! (Ex. 14:12)
- Fickleness—singing songs of victory only to fall into a heap at the very first sign of challenge (Ex. 15)
- Blasphemy
- Hatred

These are just a few I have picked, but they do serve as a lesson that we need to maybe spend less time in front of the television and more time in the Word of God! Remember, the level of your belief determines the level of God's blessing, favor, and power that you will see in your life!

TWELVE

Gladiator

*And the seventh time it happened, when the priests
blew the trumpets, that Joshua said to the people:
"Shout, for the LORD has given you the city!"*
—JOSHUA 6:16

Russell Crowe played the role of Maximus the Roman general in the five-Oscar-winning movie *Gladiator*. Before his death, Emperor Marcus Aurelius chooses Maximus to be his heir over his own son, Commodus. A power struggle ensues and Maximus and his family are condemned to death. The powerful general, who had conquered every army he had ever faced, was unable to save his family who were brutally murdered. At the sight of the charred remains of his crucified, beloved wife, he loses the will to live and allows himself to get captured and put into the Gladiator games until he dies. However, things take a dramatic turn when he realizes that he is on his way to Rome where he has the chance to rise to the top so that he will be able to look into the eyes of the man who will feel his revenge.

What fuels him? Commodus asks him the same question.

Maximus's answer: "The last words of a dying man!" Maximus lived his last breath for the last words of a dying man, his beloved emperor Marcus Aurelius, and his dream for Rome.

What do you live for? Whose words dominate your breath?

The Word of God will fuel you to live above your circumstances and live a life of purpose and power despite tragedy and opposition. This is the secret of this chapter. It's something David discovered and brought down Goliath with it. Paul and Silas discovered it and broke out of prison with it. Joshua brought down the walls of Jericho with it, and it is the key to how we open the gates of heaven to enter therein.

Make It Rain

Prayer has a voice, and praise has a shout. Don't ever reduce praise to mere vocal chords producing sounds. Praise has the power to see walls come down and chains and prison doors loosed. How? Very simply, the Bible teaches us that God inhabits the praises of His people! In fact, He not only inhabits, but He is "enthroned" in the praises of His people (Ps. 22:3). That means our praise produces a throne where the great King of kings, the Master of the universe, reigns!

Wherever God is, there freedom resides. In fact, the Bible boldly states, "Where the Spirit of the Lord is, there is liberty" (2 Cor. 3:17). That is why praise is so powerful, because it enthrones the Lord, whose very presence can bring down the walls and bust open the prisons that have held us bound!

Don't be a Christian who only praises God once the battle is over. Don't be a person who only praises the Lord in the good times. God showed Joshua in the Old Testament and Paul and Silas in the New Testament that praise is at its most potent when everything seems its bleakest!

"Praise Me for the House I Have Given You"

I was praying for a house for our family, and those words struck me like being hit in the head by a misaligned baseball pitch. "*What?* You know I would, God, but there's just one problem: You haven't given us one yet! That's why I am praying!" I felt like God must have had a very busy day dealing with famines, violence, dictators, and orphan children or something, and He had just gotten out of His timetable and schedule a little and made an oversight. Poor old God, He must have thought He had already given us the home we were believing for. Yet there we were, nine months pregnant and about to be evicted from our property because the landlord decided to sell the property, though we had been under the impression we were going to be in the property for quite some time.

To say there was pressure was an understatement. We were having our first child, and my wife, fueled by her nesting instincts, had chosen our rental property and location as the perfect locale to bring our firstborn into the world. Interestingly enough, about eleven months earlier we had a very gifted prophet come to minister at our church, and he prophesied that he saw us under incredible pressure needing things to be supplied. He went on to say that he did not know where we were currently living, but God was going to provide for us a house, and God was going to pay our school fees.

When we moved into the very nice property as tenants, my wife and a few others in the church thought perhaps that could be a fulfillment of that prophetic word, but I was convinced otherwise. I had been praying and asking God to do a miracle and help us purchase a home of our own, with no more landlords. I prayed for a place where we could come and go as we please, change the color of the walls, and do whatever made us enjoy the property more. I wanted home ownership.

So there I was, eleven months later, in the living room at about ten at night, with God asking me to praise Him for the house He had given me. *Helloooo? What house?* Leanne had gone to bed, but I felt the need to pray and press into God, as we desperately needed His intervention. We were just weeks away from having to move out so the new owners could move in. So I reminded the Almighty that I had no problem praising Him for deeds performed *when* they were performed. "I don't see no house," was my retort. Then God spoke again, *Just because you do not see it, does not mean I have not given it. Praise Me for the house I have given you!* At that word it was like a bolt of lightning went through my body and ignited hope, which replaced the fear and apprehension that had been dominating my thoughts and had prompted my prayer time.

I raced into the bedroom and woke Leanne and told her what God said. We walked out into the living room together and began to praise Him there. Then God said to me, *Not here; in Wattle Downs!* My goodness, that was the area my wife had on her wish list, but it was so far above our pay grade that it seemed like a dream. Nevertheless, I was on an obedience roll, so I packed my pregnant wife and our dog, Lulu, into the car and drove to Wattle Downs. We parked in front of a house on the water and began to praise God. *Louder!* said the Holy Spirit, so we lifted our voices to an uncomfortable volume inside of the car, my wife looking at me like I had really lost my marbles.

Get out of the car and praise Me for the home I have given you! I looked at Leanne and told her we needed to get out and stand on the front lawn of this house. As we did, again the prompting came to praise and to do so with all of our hearts. It was so embarrassing, I could imagine the angels in heaven looking down and saying, "That boy must have had some pride issues for God to humble him this way!" Then Lulu (who loved to chase cats) saw the family cat and chased it around and around the house, barking until the lights came on inside the house. *Keep praising and don't stop!* prompted the Holy Spirit, and so we did in what was becoming a feverish pitch. Then the front door opened, and a male figure silhouetted the light of the doorway.

Just then, Lulu, tired from all of her running, decided to squat right there and fertilize the man's lawn. Everything in me wanted the ground to open up and swallow me, and all the Holy Spirit kept saying was *Louder, keep praising!* It honestly was beyond embarrassing, and I thought, *This is it. My wife is going to check me into the funny farm. We are going to be arrested.* (Thank God we were not in Texas, or we may have been shot!) I could see the charges: disturbing the peace, trespassing on private property, not restraining our pet. The man stood and stared for what seemed like an eternity but was probably just thirty seconds, rubbed his eyes, and went back inside shutting the door behind him. I mean, there was a nine-month pregnant woman, her husband standing beside her, a dog fertilizing his lawn, and they were speaking in foreign languages with all their gusto and might. Maybe he thought he was dreaming, or maybe he thought it was safer inside with the door closed.

Whatever it was, as soon as he went back into the house and shut the door, it was like we were released from our burden to praise. I said to Leanne, "I think that's it. I think we can go now!" Leanne just looked at me and said, "I have never been so embarrassed in all my life!" We got into the car and drove home.

That night's nocturnal activity was flirting with insanity, and even though I was apologizing to my wife, deep down within my spirit I felt like something had shifted. Something had broken, like in Joshua's day—a "wall" had come down. The very next day, Leanne was doing the grocery shopping and met an elderly lady who attended our church who told her that her daughter was selling a home in Wattle Downs.

We drove to the home, located in a beautiful, quiet cul-de-sac. From there God began to do a series of miracles, beginning with a deposit that we did not have, then financing we were told we did not qualify for. It was just spectacular to see and be experiencing something that we certainly with all of our strength could not accomplish on our own. Praise releases the power of God into our lives and situations because it's a declaration of His majesty and sovereignty over all the earth. His power flows toward those who praise Him. I learned that evening that praise is one of the greatest ways to release God's power into a situation and push forward into what God has promised.

Just When You Think It's Over

The owner graciously allowed us to occupy the home before the close of escrow, as it seemed like such a done deal with the bank. However, I had a restlessness within my spirit that I just could not still no matter what I tried. I could not sleep one night and got up around 1:00 a.m. to pray. It felt like I had a knot in my stomach. I had felt that kind of thing before and knew it was something urgent that required intercession to bring the breakthrough! Because we had already moved in, had our little baby boy in his own crib in his own little room, not to mention my wife had already torn up the carpets and begun ripping down the wallpaper, I prayed with all my might, declaring the promises of God and thanking Him for His faithfulness and loving-kindness.

The next day, the bank called me at work and said that there had been a problem with the mortgage insurance. Our earnings being so little had put the bank in a precarious position that the insurance company felt was too great a risk. In their estimation, there was no way we would be able to repay the loan on our salary. I hung up the phone and it was like a knife had gone right into my gut. I thought to myself, *They are one hundred percent correct, our salary is so small, who was I to believe we could do this?*

I drove home, and as I walked into the front door Leanne proudly showed me the progress she had made that day on removing what was left of the previous tenants' flooring and wall coverings. I glanced over to the side of the room where my little boy was lying in his rocker, snug in his little pajamas in front of the little heater we had bought. I did not know how to tell Leanne what had transpired that day. It would be a burden too heavy for her, so I decided to carry it alone. That night again around midnight, I slipped out of bed, braving the cold as a gusty southerly wind swept through the cul-de-sac like a runaway locomotive. I made my way down to the harbor where I loved to go and pray, and as I prayed I saw a boat on the water being tossed by the waves. My immediate thought was, *Who is nuts enough to be out on a night like this?* Just then I saw a man walking on the water toward the boat, and I realized it was a vision. I kept watching as the lone water walker (who I knew to be Jesus) stopped about thirty feet or so from the boat. He then beckoned with His hand toward the boat, and I saw one of the passengers get out of the boat and walk on the stormy water toward Jesus. A little beyond the halfway point, I saw the man (who I knew to be Peter) become frantic as he lost his balance and began to sink. Just then I saw Jesus lunge at him and grab him by the arm, lifting him back up onto the water, and the two of them walked back to the boat and got in. Then Jesus said to me, *Even if your faith fails, I am there to catch you and lift you up!*

The bank manager told me he would negotiate on our behalf with the mortgage insurance companies and would call at around four in the afternoon with the news. I waited with bated breath for the phone to ring, and as it reached four, that same knot I had in my stomach the night before felt like it was amplified 100-fold. I tried to dismiss it, pleading with Jesus to make it all right, but the knot in my gut told me otherwise—we were going to be denied. When the phone finally rang, I just stared at it, frozen, as if paralyzed for a moment. I was caught between wanting to hear the bank manager say he was successful and it had all been nothing but a bad dream, and the inevitable words, "I'm sorry, you've been denied." As I picked up the phone it felt like it was made of lead, so heavy in my hand, and then the bank manager confirmed what I had felt. We were denied. There was nothing more he could do. We could not buy the house.

How was I going to tell Leanne? Where would we go? My little baby boy, completely dependent upon my provision and yet totally unaware of the ramifications of what I had just been told, would have to move elsewhere. What would we do? Just then the same voice that said to me, *Even if your faith fails, I am there to pick you up,* said to me, *Watch what I am about to do!* I needed a miracle, and I needed it right then. Though everything in the natural world was chaos, I had such a peace at the words He spoke to me.

I had to call the owner and tell them what had transpired. I didn't want to do it because we would have to pay for damages, as we had ripped up the old carpet and terrorized the walls. As the phone rang I had a lump in my throat; I was afraid I wouldn't be able to speak at all when they answered. I then told the father of the owner of the property what the bank had said. The daughter selling the property was overseas and had given power of attorney to sell the home to her dad. He was very stoic, nonchalant, and matter-of-fact on the phone. He growled, "Well, you had better come around here and talk about what we should do from here!" I drove over to his house, once again feelings of embarrassment washing over me, only interrupted by feelings of despair about what I would tell Leanne. Just as I pulled up to the front of the house the words came to me again: *Watch what I am about to do!*

I walked in and was greeted rather neutrally—it wasn't cold, but it certainly wasn't a "welcoming an old friend" kind of greeting either. The father told me to sit on the couch and bring him up to speed on where things were with the deal. When I finished, he just sat there silently, staring off into a distant place. Then he broke the silence by saying gruffly, "Is there no one else who would fund you?" I said there was one other place, but they needed a much larger deposit. "How much larger?" he barked, demanding to know. I replied that the lender wanted almost double the deposit. Again, he stared off into the distance like he was looking for something he had lost. "Wait here for a moment," he said in a steely tone, and with that he got up and walked out of the room.

I sat there, a cocktail of emotions running rampant. What was I going to tell Leanne? How embarrassing. And how was I going to tell the man, "Oh, and besides not being able to purchase the home, we also took advantage of your generosity in letting us move in early by vandalizing the floors and walls." Again, the words from Christ came: *Watch what I am about to do. When your faith fails, I am there to lift you up!*

Just then the door opened and he returned. He sat on the sofa opposite me and said, "When we moved to New Zealand from England many years ago, Joan, my wife, was pregnant with our first. We didn't have the money to buy a home, but I had made friends with a builder, and the commission he got from building one of the homes he gave to me so I could buy the home for our family-to-be. All my life, I've been waiting to do that for someone else. How short did you say you were to qualify for the loan?" I told him, and he reached into his pocket and pulled out the biggest wad of $100 bills I had ever seen in my life. He began to slam them down on the coffee table, counting them until he reached the amount we needed.

I cried all the way home. God was true to His word and magnificently faithful, fulfilling His promise when I was willing to push in praise and in intercessory prayer. I cannot explain to you the euphoria I experienced the next day as I walked into the bank and asked to see the loan manager, presenting the bounty of $100 bills I had just received and seeing the expression on his face. Deeds were written up, contracts exchanged, and we got a home in Wattle Downs! Even if your faith fails, He is there to carry you and pick you up. You just need to learn the power of praise and see how it will push you into the great things God has set aside for you!

It's Always Praise Time

Too many people think that praise is reserved for rewarding God for a job well done and not before. Because we have been brought up in a dysfunctional world of performance-based acceptance, we treat God the same way our parents treated us. When we did well, we were praised; but when we did poorly we were scolded or ignored. But God is good all the time, and even though you and I may be facing a storm, we must remember the words of the psalmist: "The LORD sat enthroned at the Flood" (Ps. 29:10). Faith is praising God for His goodness when you don't see it, for His loving-kindness when you don't feel it, and for His faithfulness when you haven't yet received it!

Paul and Silas were beaten and imprisoned, but in the midnight hour they began to praise God, not because they were promised parole, not because they were getting a new house, but because He is God and worthy of all our praise. If we praise Him only when *we feel good,* then we make a statement that our good feelings trump His majesty. But when we learn to praise Him despite how we may feel—good, bad, or indifferent—then we see His power come flooding into our lives, not only delivering us but blessing those around us! Be a perpetual praiser, and you are going to see the best God has for you flood your life! Praise Him! He is worthy! So the psalmist says in Psalm 150!

Bring Down the Walls

Are you facing some walls at the moment? Are you looking at insurmountable odds that are stacked against you? Well, first find out what God's Word says about your situation and then begin to praise Him. Because if He said it, He will also perform it. He is not a man that He should lie! Be like Joshua at Jericho and bring those walls down! Praise your way forward. Not only will you advance but you will feel better too. Did you know that praising people are the happiest people? Did you know that praise brings you closer to God? Psalm 100:4 says, "Enter into His gates with thanksgiving, and into His courts with praise!"

Your body was designed to praise God. When you do this you are like a fish in the water or a bird in the air—you are in your perfect environment. All kinds of wonderful endorphins are released in your body that make you a happier person, and your spirit and soul will soar because praise is rooted in the character of God, who is so good, so loving, so gracious, so forgiving, so merciful, so generous, so present, and so amazing! Take five minutes now and begin to praise Him for what He has done, what He is doing, and what He has yet to do in your life!

Closing Thoughts

As I sit here about to fire this final edit off to the publisher, I am reminded how much of a PUSH this book required, three computers and six losses of the manuscript. It certainly wasn't an easy task.

Nothing in my life has come to me easily. In fact, as my mother used to say, "Easy come, easy go." Things that come easily to us also seem to leave us just as quickly as they arrive. I find the faith and battle required to get something generates both appreciation and security for that object.

There is nothing more powerful in the universe than the Word of God. When we align our lives with His Word powerful things happen. All effective prayer occurs when we pray from a word of God in our hearts that flows from our mouths.

Strike the Ground, Open Heaven

Praying with passion is paramount to producing powerful results. Bartimaeus arrested the attention of the Messiah as He passed by because of his passionate crying out, refusing to adhere to the status quo. However, not all people in the Bible who were in desperate need of a breakthrough approached it with passion. One in particular is King Joash, who came down to Elisha, the man of God, in a time of great national distress, while Elisha, lying on his deathbed, was moments away from slipping out of this life and into eternity.

In the story found in 2 Kings 13, King Joash came to Elisha the prophet to seek assistance from the Lord because the much mightier Syrian army had surrounded the city and laid siege against it. Elisha spoke God's word of deliverance and commanded the king to strike the ground with the handful of arrows he had grasped in his hand. The Bible says the king struck three times and stopped. Elisha became angry with the king and said, "Why did you only strike three times and stop? Why did you not strike five or six times? For then you would have defeated the Syrians. But now you will only strike them three times and then they will regroup and overrun you."

When we pray, we must learn to "pray through," or pray until completion. Don't give up halfway through. Don't stop short and hope that there is enough momentum to get you across the line. Pray through until you have the breakthrough. That is PUSH prayer.

I just got hit with bronchitis like I have never been hit before. My doctor told me it's because people don't complete their prescription of antibiotics, so the disease or germ, which is almost defeated, survives and rebuilds itself with immunity against that strain of antibiotic. Each year the bronchitis seems to get more obstinate. This means next time you are going to have to use a much stronger antibiotic because the new strain of bronchitis has become resistant to the previous type.

Likewise, God instructs us to finish the job, to pray *until* we see the victory.

God is for you. He is waiting on an invitation to move powerfully in your world. There is a devil, whom you need not fear because Christ has completely defeated him. Even though there are forces resisting God's perfect will from coming to pass in your life, you can PUSH with the weight and power of the Word of God behind you into all that God has for you, and see heaven come to earth in your life.

God bless you as you PUSH!

Notes

Introduction

1. Loraine Boettner, *The Reformed Doctrine of Predestination* (Phillipsburg, NJ: P&R Publishing, 1932), 105.

Chapter 3

1. http://webarchive.nationalarchives.gov.uk/+/http:/www.home office.gov.uk/documents/paying_the_price.pdf?view=Binary
2. "God After the Death of God," Richard L. Rubenstein, *After Auschwitz: History, Theology, and Contemporary Judaism,* 2nd. ed. (Baltimore: Johns Hopkins University Press, 1992), 293–306, and "Is God Dead?" *TIME* magazine, April 8, 1966.
3. http://www.lyricsfreak.com/a/abba/the+winner+takes+it+all _20002664.html
4. http://www.bartleby.com/42/634.html

Chapter 4

1. T. C. N. Singh, "On the Effect of Music and Dance on Plants," Bihar *Agricultural College* magazine, Volume 13, no. 1, 1962–1963.

Chapter 7

1. John O'Hara, Appointment in Samarra (Penguin Classics: New York, 2013).
2. "Republican Senate candidate defends rape comment, expresses regret for phrasing," http://www.foxnews.com/politics/2012/10/23/god-at-work-when-rape-leads-to-pregnancy-indiana-republican-senate-candidate/

Chapter 8

1. ThinkExist.com/quotes/Einstein
2. Thinkexist.com/Quotes/Einstein
3. Albert Einstein, *The World as I See It* (Philosophical Library: New York, 1949), 24–28, and *New York Times* magazine, November 9, 1930, 1–4. Reprinted in *Ideas and Opinions*, (Crown Publishers, Inc.: New York, 1954), 36–40.
4. Martin Luther, *On the Bondage of the Will*, 1525.

Chapter 9

1. Christian Classics Etheral Library, "Selcet Sermons: Sinners in the Hands of an Angry God," http://www.ccel.org/ccel/edwards/sermons.sinners.html.

About the Author

Jurgen Matthesius is the founder of C3 San Diego, a thriving, life-giving church in two locations (soon to be four) in the heart of San Diego.

He is the author of *God in Hollywood*, an Australian best-seller, and *Walk on Water*. He is also seen across the world through the church's podcasts, as well as in regular TV spots on TBN, SHINE, and Daystar. Jurgen is a frequent speaker at both Christian and non-religious conferences and meetings. He also served as a consultant to leading businesspeople, celebrities, and athletes.

Pastor Jurgen and his wife, Leanne, serve together in San Diego, where they live with their daughter (Zoe Abigail) and three sons (Jordan, Ashley, and Tommy).